ISBN: 978-1-8382809-6-3

Published by:

City of Newcastle Upon Tyne
Newcastle Libraries
Tyne Bridge Publishing, 2021
unless otherwise indicated

The River Coquet

A Personal Portrait of the Birds, Wildlife and History

MiE Fielding

This book is dedicated to my wife Darlene for her love, support and encouragement.

Goshawk, at Holystone Common. Although numbers have increased in recent years, they are still a rare sight. Look for Goshawk on a windy day in March when they can often be seen displaying.

Painting mixed media on board 2017.

If life were like a day in June
And we had choice of England wide
who would not spend an afternoon
and evening too, by Coquetside.

The Coquet for ever! The Coquet for aye!
The Coquet, the king o' the stream an the brae.
Frae his high mountain throne to his bed in the sea
Oh! where shall we find such a river as he.

Map showing the route of the River Coquet running west to east from its
source in the Northumberland National Park to the North Sea at Amble.

Contents

Introduction

The River Coquet (designated a Site of Special Scientific Interest, SSSI), the most famous of all Northumberland's trouting rivers and many say the most beautiful, bisects the county from west to east for a distance of some 57 miles, its loops and twists spelling out its name according to country folk. From its source, the windswept border country of Brownhart Law in the Cheviots, the river passes the picturesque villages of Alwinton, Harbottle, Holystone, Hepple, Thropton, Rothbury, Felton and Warkworth, before its waters empty into the North Sea at Amble, opposite the RSPB reserve of Coquet Island.

For the visiting birdwatcher, the sheer variety of habitats along the river's course and the spectacular birdlife of Coquet Island, means that all of Northumberland's birdlife, with a few exceptions, can be found in this one easily explorable area. Opened in 2006, The St Oswald's Way is a 97-mile long-distance walking route exploring some of the finest stretches of the Northumberland coastline and upland landscapes. From the Holy Island of Lindisfarne in the north, St Oswald's Way follows the coast as far south as Warkworth before heading inland along the Coquet valley to Rothbury, finally ending at Heavenfield on Hadrian's Wall.

Since 2000, Coquetdale's wildlife and its resident riverine bird populations have remained relatively stable, however, it is our farmland and migrant birds that have shown the most marked declines. In the UK as a whole, farmland birds have declined by a staggering 48% since the 1970s.

Corn Bunting is now extinct in Northumberland, with Grey Partridge, Lapwing, and Skylark, amongst other species, showing worrying downward population trends. There are many reasons for this decline - climate change, farming practices and particularly house building, which has no provision for nesting species such as House Sparrow, Common Starling, Common Swift, House Martin etc. These characterless housing estates, which are more profitable for the developers, are now engulfing traditional farmland at an alarming rate. Other factors include hedge and tree 'netting', used by these same developers to 'discourage' nest building during construction. Barns and other farm buildings converted to residential use has also contributed to the decline in Barn Swallows and other species, including bats.

It is now urgent that we double our efforts to protect and enhance our once varied and beautiful countryside and I have outlined some of the many conservation societies and voluntary organisations at the end of this book.

MiE Fielding

My garden isn't for me
It's for all the lives we push to the margins
And that are waiting for a rebirth of compassion.

Benjamin Vogt

Corn Bunting, now sadly extinct in Northumberland.
How I miss those 'jangling keys' in the summer air.

Notes for Visitors

Where to stay. There are many different types and standards of accommodation along the length of the River Coquet and full information can be obtained from local tourist information centres and websites. Details at the back of this book.

Public transport is provided (at the time of writing) by Arriva bus services with service X18 and X20 covering the coastal runs (Amble, Warkworth etc) and service X15 running from Newcastle via Morpeth to Felton village/Alnwick and Berwick-upon-Tweed. Service 16 covers Rothbury, Thropton, Holystone, Harbottle and Awinton, operated by Spirit Bus Services. Addresses at the back of this book. The nearest railway station is Alnmouth then bus service X18 to Warkworth/Amble. There is a railway station at Widdrington where it is possible to take a bus to Red Row and then walk to the Druridge Bay sites (East Chevington, Druridge Pools etc).

By car. A word of caution. Upper Coquetdale is a very rural and remote area. Around the year 2000 there was possibly 12+ service stations where petrol or diesel could be obtained. That situation has changed dramatically as it has done throughout the UK. Small independent garages have virtually disappeared and supply is dominated by supermarket chains. Fuel can be obtained from Alnwick, Morpeth and Amble with no fuel available in the entire Coquetdale region. Check your tank before visiting. It is worth remembering that a journey from Amble to Barrow Burn via Rothbury and back is around 70 miles (112km). At the time of writing electric vehicle charging points are limited.

Rights of way and access. Boundaries, rights of way etc, are always subject to change and information in this book should not be used without checking relevant maps and with organisations such as the RSPB (for Coquet Island) and the Ministry of Defence if visitors intend to walk on the Otterburn ranges. Some sites require a permit or a fee is payable.

Reed Bunting at Caistron.

8

Early spring in Upper Coquetdale with a covering of snow still lying on higher ground. Sharpe's Folly at Whitton near Rothbury is in the foreground.

The Countryside Code

Updated Version 4 - October 2016

Respect other people

Please respect the local community and other people using the outdoors. Remember your actions can affect people's lives and livelihoods.

Consider the local community and other people enjoying the outdoors

Respect the needs of local people and visitors alike – for example, don't block gateways, driveways or other paths with your vehicle. When riding a bike or driving a vehicle, slow down or stop for horses, walkers and farm animals and give them plenty of room. By law, cyclists must give way to walkers and horse riders on bridleways.

Co-operate with people at work in the countryside. For example, keep out of the way when farm animals are being gathered or moved and follow directions from the farmer. Busy traffic on small country roads can be unpleasant and dangerous to local people, visitors and wildlife - so slow down and, where possible, leave your vehicle at home. Consider sharing lifts and use alternatives such as public transport or cycling. For public transport information, phone Traveline on 0871 200 22 33 or visit www.traveline.info.

The Coquet Estuary with Warkworth Castle in the distance.

Leave gates and property as you find them and follow paths unless wider access is available

A farmer will normally close gates to keep farm animals in but may sometimes leave them open so the animals can reach food and water. Leave gates as you find them or follow instructions on signs. When in a group, make sure the last person knows how to leave the gates.

Follow paths unless wider access is available, such as on open country or registered common land (known as 'open access land'). If you think a sign is illegal or misleading such as a 'Private - No Entry' sign on a public path, contact the local authority.

Leave machinery and farm animals alone. Don't interfere with animals even if you think they are in distress. Try to alert the farmer instead. Use gates, stiles or gaps in field boundaries if you can – climbing over walls, hedges and fences can damage them and increase the risk of farm animals escaping.
Our heritage matters to all of us – be careful not to disturb ruins and historic sites.

Protect the natural environment

We all have a responsibility to protect the countryside now and for future generations, so make sure you don't harm animals, birds, plants or trees and try to leave no trace of your visit. When out with your dog make sure it is not a danger or nuisance to farm animals, horses, wildlife or other people.

Blackcap (male).

Leave no trace of your visit and take your litter home.

Protecting the natural environment means taking special care not to damage, destroy or remove features such as rocks, plants and trees. They provide homes and food for wildlife and add to everybody's enjoyment of the countryside. Litter and leftover food doesn't just spoil the beauty of the countryside, it can be dangerous to wildlife and farm animals – so take your litter home with you.

Fires can be as devastating to wildlife and habitats as they are to people and property – so be careful with naked flames and cigarettes at any time of the year. Sometimes controlled fires are used to manage vegetation, particularly on heaths and moors between 1 October and 15 April, but if a fire appears to be unattended report it by calling 999.

Keep dogs under effective control.

When you take your dog outdoors, always ensure it does not disturb wildlife, farm animals, horses or other people by keeping it under effective control. This means that you:
• keep your dog on a lead, or
• keep it in sight at all times, be aware of what it's doing and be confident it will return to you promptly on command.
• ensure it does not stray off the path or area where you have a right of access. Special dog rules may apply in particular situations, so always look out for local signs – for example:
• dogs may be banned from certain areas that people use, or there may be restrictions, byelaws or control orders limiting where they can go.
• the access rights that normally apply to open country and registered common land (known as 'open access' land) require dogs to be kept on a short lead between 1 March and 31 July, to help protect ground nesting birds, and all year round near farm animals.
• at the coast, there may also be some local restrictions that require dogs to be kept on a short lead during the bird breeding season, and to prevent disturbance to flocks of resting and feeding birds during other times of year. it's always good practice (and a legal requirement on 'open access' land) to keep your dog on a lead around farm animals and horses, for your own safety and for the welfare of the animals. A farmer may shoot a dog that is attacking or chasing farm animals without being liable to compensate the dog's owner. However, if cattle or horses chase you and your dog, it is safer to let your dog off the lead – don't risk getting hurt by trying to protect it. Your dog will be much safer if you let it run away from a farm animal in these circumstances and so will you.

Everyone knows how unpleasant dog mess is and it can cause infections, so always clean up after your dog and get rid of the mess responsibly – 'bag it and bin it'. Make sure your dog is wormed regularly to protect it, other animals and people.

Enjoy the outdoors

Even when going out locally, it's best to get the latest information about where and when you can go. For example, your rights to go onto some areas of open access land and coastal land may be restricted in particular places at particular times. Find out as much as you can about where you are going.

Plan ahead and be prepared

You'll get more from your visit if you refer to up-to-date maps or guidebooks and websites before you go. Visit Natural England on GOV.UK or contact local information centres or libraries for a list of outdoor recreation groups offering advice on specialist activities.

You're responsible for your own safety and for others in your care – especially children - so be prepared for natural hazards, changes in weather and other events. Wild animals, farm animals and horses can behave unpredictably if you get too close, especially if they're with their young - so give them space.

Check weather forecasts before you leave. Conditions can change rapidly, especially on mountains and along the coast, so don't be afraid to turn back. When visiting the coast check for tide times on EasyTide - don't risk getting cut off by rising tides and take care on slippery rocks and seaweed.

Part of the appeal of the countryside is that you can get away from it all. You may not see anyone for hours, and there are many places without clear mobile phone signals, so let someone else know where you're going and when you expect to return.

Follow advice and local signs

England has about 190,000 km (118,000 miles) of public rights of way, providing many opportunities to enjoy the natural environment. Get to know the signs and symbols used in the countryside to show paths and open countryside. See the Countryside Code leaflet for some of the symbols you may come across.

The Birdwatchers' Code of Conduct

Following the birdwatchers' code is good practice, common sense and should enable us all to enjoy seeing birds. Some three million adults go birdwatching every year in the UK*. The code puts the interests of birds first and respects other people, whether or not they are interested in birds.

It applies not just when you are at a nature reserve, but whenever you are watching birds in the UK or abroad. It has been produced by the leading bird organisations, magazines and websites. It will be most effective if we lead by example and sensitively challenge the minority of birdwatchers who behave inappropriately.

The interests of birds come first.

Birds respond to people in many ways, depending on the species, location and time of year. Disturbance can keep birds from their nests, leaving chicks hungry or enabling predators to take eggs or young.

During cold weather or when migrants have just made a long flight, repeatedly flushing birds can mean they use up vital energy that they need for feeding. Intentional or reckless disturbance of some species at or near the nest is illegal in Britain.

Whether your particular interest is photography, ringing, sound recording or birdwatching, remember that the interests of the bird must always come first.
• Avoid going too close to birds or disturbing their habitats – if a bird flies away or makes repeated alarm calls, you're too close. And if it leaves, you won't get a good view.
• Stay on roads and paths where they exist and avoid disturbing habitat used by birds.
• Think about your fieldcraft. Disturbance is not just about going too close – a flock of wading birds on the foreshore can be disturbed from a mile away if you stand on the seawall.
• Repeatedly playing a recording of birdsong or calls to encourage a bird to respond can divert a territorial bird from other important duties, such as feeding its young. Never use playback to attract a species during its breeding season. See Birds, habitats and the law (linked from this page) in relation to Schedule 1 species in the UK.

Be an ambassador for birdwatching

Think about your fieldcraft and behaviour, not just so that you can enjoy your birdwatching, but so others can too.

Respond positively to questions from interested passers-by. They may not be birdwatchers yet, but a good view of a bird or a helpful answer may light a spark of interest. Your enthusiasm could start a lifetime's interest in birds and a greater appreciation of wildlife and its conservation.

Consider using local services, such as pubs, restaurants and petrol stations, and public transport. Raising awareness of the benefits to local communities of trade from visiting birdwatchers may, ultimately, help the birds themselves.

Birds, habitats and the law

Laws protecting birds and their habitats have helped to secure the conservation of many species. They are the result of hard campaigning by generations of birdwatchers. We must make sure that they are adhered to.

What to do if you find a rare bird

If you discover a rare bird, please bear the following in mind:
• Consider the potential impact of spreading the news and make an effort to inform the landowner (or, on a nature reserve, the warden) first. Think about whether the site can cope with a large number of visitors and whether sensitive species, such as breeding terns, flocks of wading birds or rare plants, might be at risk. The County Bird Recorder or another experienced birdwatcher can often give good advice.
• On private land, always talk to the landowner first. With a little planning, access can often be arranged.
• 'Twitches' can raise money for a local reserve, other wildlife project or charity. Consider organising a voluntary collection at access points to the site.
• Rare breeding birds are at risk from egg-collectors and some birds of prey from persecution. If you discover a rare breeding species that you think is vulnerable, contact the RSPB, which has considerable experience in protecting rare breeding birds, and report it to the County Bird Recorder or the Rare Breeding Birds Panel (websites linked from this page). Also, consider telling the landowner – in most cases, this will ensure that the nest is not disturbed accidentally.

Some useful guidelines

If you have the opportunity to see a rare bird, enjoy it, but don't let your enthusiasm override common sense.
In addition to the guidelines above:
• If you go to see a rare bird, park sensibly, follow instructions and consider making a donation if requested.
• Don't get too close for a photograph – you'll earn the wrath of everyone else if you flush the bird out of sight.

Birdlife International top 10 tips on how to be a good birdwatcher

1. Dress for the occasion

Imagine going to school in your pyjamas or playing tennis in a suit and tie. Pretty weird, right? Every activity has an appropriate type of clothing, and birdwatching is no exception. Try to wear dark, camouflaged colours so that birds don't see you coming. And no matter what the weather's like, make sure you bring clothes that will keep you warm, dry and protected from the sun – you may find yourself observing the birds in fascination for longer than you expected.

2. Pack your birdwatching bag

No good birdwatcher leaves the house without these key items in their bag: a pair of binoculars (any brand will do), a pen and paper to record their sightings, and a bird guide. Make sure to learn the words and expressions that bird guides use: it makes identification much easier. And don't forget to bring drinks and snacks – birdwatching is thirsty work. You may also want to take a camera but remember to turn off the flash (see the next point).

3. Avoid disturbing birds

Imagine you're a Common Cuckoo (Cuculus canorus) that has just migrated 8,000 kilometres from Angola to the UK. You land on a branch, desperate to find some insects to eat and get some rest. Suddenly, a loud group of humans rushes towards you. Oh no! Predators! You spread your weary wings and take to the skies once again. Always remember that the safety and welfare of the birds comes first. Scaring birds stresses them out and stops them from feeding, breeding and resting. Instead, walk slowly and softly, speak quietly, put your phone on silent and, above all, don't get too close – that's what your binoculars are for! All you need to do is find a good place to sit, be patient, and let the birds come to you. Birds are always a lot more fun to watch when they're not flying away in fright.

4. Leave nests in peace

Any parent will tell you that looking after babies is hard work. When it comes to bird breeding grounds, it's especially important to keep your distance. Disturbing a nest can cause the parents to fly away, leaving chicks hungry with nobody to feed them, or exposing the eggs or chicks to predators. If you hang around a nest for too long, the parents may become so wary that they abandon it altogether. The best thing you can do if you come across a nest is to walk away quietly.

5. Use bird hides
Bird hides and observation towers are the ultimate "life hack", allowing you to get a great view of birds without making your presence known. They're also the perfect place to shelter from the sun or huddle with a flask of hot chocolate on wet and windy days. You'll be surprised at how many bird hides are out there – have a quick search online to see if there's one near you.

6. Follow the laws of the land
Whether you're going round to your friend's house for dinner or going out birdwatching, it's always important to be a good guest. Remember to be considerate to the people who own the land that you're visiting. Close all gates behind you, stick to the path and never trespass on private land – you don't want to give birdwatchers a bad reputation!

7. Leave no trace
Go by the motto: "take nothing and leave nothing behind". Never drop litter or trample over vegetation – you may be damaging the homes of the birds you're trying to watch.

8. Look for birds everywhere
Think cities don't have birds? Think again! Birds are everywhere once you start looking. Think outside the box when searching for birdwatching spots: parks, churchyards, market squares, canals and even rooftops all hold surprises.

9. No birds? No problem!
Even seasoned birdwatchers have bad days. If you set out brimming with excitement, only to find that all the birds in the area have decided to spend the day somewhere else, don't get disheartened. Try listening rather than looking. There are lots of great birdsong identification apps to help you, and soon, you'll be able to do it all by yourself.

10. Spread the joy!
When you're out and about with your binoculars and bird book, passers-by might be interested in what you're doing. Be an ambassador for birdwatching: take the time to explain and share with them your most interesting sightings. You might inspire them to follow your lead and become birdwatchers too!

Birds of Upper Coquetdale
Status 1903

The following extract from '*Upper Coquetdale*' by D D Dixon acts as a useful comparison with the current state of the biodiversity in the area.

Corvinae: **The Raven:** Seen occasionally; it has bred in recent years at Rough Castles and Ravensheugh. **Carrion Crow**: Resident, fairly plentiful. **Hooded Crow:** Winter visitor (but has bred once at Rough Castles), rather plentiful. **Jackdaw**: Abundant. **Rook:** Plentiful. **Magpie:** Seen occasionally. **Jay:** Scarce.

Falconidae: **The Peregrine:** Seen occasionally, bred in recent years at Keyheugh and Hepple. **Sparrowhawk**: Resident rather plentiful. **Kestrel:** Resident and plentiful. **Merlin**: Still breeds near Debdon, fairly plentiful. **Common Buzzard:** Has occurred on the moors.

Barn owl by Thomas Bewick

Ardeidae: **The Heron:** Plentiful, breeds at Harbottle. **Stringdae;- The Barn Owl:** Rather scarce. **Long and Short-Eared-Owl:** Fairly plentiful. Tawny Owl plentiful.

Anatidae: **Common Wild Duck**: Plentiful. **Teal duck:** Rather scarce. **Widgeon:** Occurs occasionally. **Pochard**: Winter visitor occurs on Cragside lakes. **Goldeneye**: Winter visitor occurs on the Coquet and Cragside lakes, scarce. **Goosander**: Winter visitor seen in small flocks on the Coquet and Cragside lakes.

Columbidae: **Ring Dove**: Resident and plentiful. **Stock Dove:** Winter visitor and scarce. **Rock Dove:** breeds in the district.

Culculidae: **Cuckoo**: A spring migrant and plentiful.
Rallidae: **Corncrake**: Spring visitant, fairly plentiful. **Waterhen**: Plentiful

resident. **Water Rail**: Seen occasionally in winter on River Coquet. **The Coot:** Also breeds in the district.

Charadriidae: **Lapwing:** Plentiful. **Golden Plover:** Breeds on the moors, plentiful. **Ringed Plover:** Breeds on the Coquet and on Cragside lakes occasionally.

Scolopacidae: **The Woodcock**: Resident now known to breed freely in the district. **Common Snipe**: Resident and plentiful. **Jack Snipe**, winter migrant, plentiful during some winters. **Sandpiper**: Spring visitor and plentiful. **Redshank**: Spring visitant, breeds on the Coquet and Cragside lakes. **Curlew**: Spring visitant, breeds on the moors.

Spotted Flycatcher, now a red listed species of conservation concern with a UK population decline of 89% since 1967. D D Dixon notes in 1903 that they are 'plentiful' at Cragside. Drawn by the author in 1994.

Larridae: **Black-headed Gull**: Breeds in the district notably at Selby's lake and Fallowlees, has bred at Cragside. **Herring Gull**: Has bred at Cragside lakes.

Podicipepidae: **Little Grebe**: Resident and scarce.
Alcidinidae: **Kingfisher**: Resident fairly plentiful.
Caprimulgidae: **Nightjar**: Spring visitant, plentiful. 'An exceedingly useful bird, destroying large quantities of moths and beetles'.

Cypselidae: **Swift:** Spring visitant, fairly plentiful.

Sturninae: **Starling:** Abundant. Thousands roosting amongst the rhododendrons in Cragside grounds. 'It is a most interesting sight watching them go to roost in the evening'.

Emberizinae: **Black-headed Bunting*:** Resident and fairly plentiful. **Yellow Bunting:** Spring visitor and plentiful. **Reed Bunting:** Spring visitant, fairly plentiful. **Snow Bunting:** Winter visitant fairly plentiful.

Fringillanae: **Goldfinch:** Winter visitant, not so plentiful as in former years. **Siskin:** Pretty little bird, winter visitant and scarce. **Greenfinch:** Resident and plentiful. **House Sparrow:** Resident and abundant. **Tree Sparrow:** Resident and fairly plentiful. **Chaffinch:** Resident and plentiful. **Linnet:** Spring visitant fairly plentiful. **Lesser Redpoll:** Resident species, very plentiful in grounds at Cragside. **Bullfinch:** Also resident and plentiful.

Blackbird or 'Black Ouzel' by Thomas Berwick

Hirundininae: **Chimney Swallow, House Martin** and **Sand Martin** are all plentiful as spring migrants.

Certhinae: **Tree Creeper:** Resident and plentiful.

Muscicapinae: **Spotted Flycatcher:** Spring migrant, plentiful at Cragside.

Ampelinae: **Waxwing:** An occasional winter visitor.
Montacallinae: **Pied and Grey Wagtail:** Plentiful. **Meadow Pipit** and **Tree Pipit** fairly plentiful.

Parinae: **Long-tailed Tit, Coal Tit, Great Tit, Marsh Tit** and **Blue Tit** all plentiful.

Cinclinae: **Dipper**: Plentiful.

Accentorinae: **Hedge Sparrow**: Plentiful.

Turdinae: **Missel Thrush** and **Song Thrush** plentiful. **Redwing** and **Fieldfares** plentiful in winter. **Common blackbird**: Resident and plentiful. Ring Ouzel, a spring migrant of this district, fairly plentiful. **Whinchat** and **Stonechat**, fairly plentiful spring migrants. **Robin:** is resident and plentiful. **Blackcap Warbler**: **Garden Warbler**, **Chiff-Chaff**, **Willow Wren**, and **Wood Wren**, as spring migrants plentiful in Cragside grounds.

Picidae: **Greater** and **Lesser Spotted Woodpeckers** have both occurred in the district.

Phasianadae: **Common Pheasant** and **Partridge** abound, also **Red Grouse** and **Black Grouse** being fairly plentiful.

Pelecanidae: The **Gannet** or **Solan Goose** has occurred in the district. A fine specimen being in the possession of Mr Richard Murray of the Chirnhills, near Rothbury, having been caught by a shepherd's dog about Coquet head and preserved by Mr Murray. **Pallas's Sandgrouse** ** has occurred in the district, one specimen being picked up at Cragside about 15 years ago (1888) and sent to the Natural History Museum in Newcastle upon Tyne, by the late Lord Armstrong. It had struck a telegraph wire. The **Little Auk** has occurred on the Coquet, a specimen having been taken at Rothbury a few years ago. **Great Northern Diver** has also occurred near Rothbury and also on the Blackburn lake at Cragside. **Lesser White-fronted Goose** has occurred at Cragside, the writer having shot 3, two of which were preserved and are in the possession of Lord Armstrong. The **Dotterel** breeds on the Coquet in the Rothbury district. The **Little Tern** has occurred at Cragside, one having been picked up dead about 5 years ago and a **Great Grey Shrike** was seen carrying prey in its talons on 2nd November 1903.

———————————————

An amazing account! One can only wonder what kind of 'lively discussion' this would cause had it appeared on social media these days. *Black-headed Bunting" was a common name given to Reed Bunting although the later species is also mentioned. The 'first' Black-headed Bunting was recorded or rather 'shot' (as was the Victorian way) on November 3rd, 1868, near Brighton Sussex. ** There was a minor invasion of Pallas's Sand Grouse in 1859, followed by a greater invasion in 1863, and again in 1888.

Reed Bunting.   _Pastel by the author, 1998._

When to Visit

Spring: 'Late April early May can be excellent for birdwatching at any location throughout Britain and at this time of the year the River Coquet is no exception. Visitors to the area can explore its birdwatching locations with the knowledge that the number of visible species will be at its greatest with many winter visitors lingering on into May, being joined by others that have spent the cold winter months in much warmer climes. A trip around Coquet Island, for example, might well produce divers and grebes as well as the expected terns.

Holystone Woods.

Likewise inland, Redwing and Fieldfare are often seen in May, indeed there are several summer records of Fieldfare (a winter visitor). One was found as the prey of a Merlin on June 29!

May is a splendid time to practise birdsong recognition* and the dale woodlands, such as Holystone (pictured above), are alive with sound, as are the moors of Upper Coquetdale.

In recent years there has been a plethora of bird song identification apps produced for mobile phones, some good, some terrible. Whilst they can useful, please do not be tempted to try to lure birds closer by using these apps. It can be distressing for birds.

Late summer and autumn: The coastal locations of the Coquet Estuary and Hauxley are at their most interesting with an abundance of Terns and returning passage waders. This is the best time to see the rare Roseate Tern, as they leave their breeding site on nearby Coquet Island, often to roost and preen with the more numerous common, Arctic and Sandwich Terns. Autumn can produce spectacular coastal movements of Skuas. Arctic Skua can often be seen pirating sand eels from terns above holidaymakers' heads on Warkworth beach!

Wryneck, a rare autumn migrant.

Lapwing, Golden Plover and Curlew return to the estuary from Upper Coquetdale and can be joined by passage waders such as Curlew Sandpiper, Greenshank, Whimbrel and Little Stint. At Caistron, inland passage waders can be joined by Black Tern, Osprey or Hobby. September through to November is rarity time. Some of Britain's rarest birds have been discovered on the Northumbrian coast, such as the Wryneck (pictured).

Every year, 'falls' of migrants appear. Goldcrests, Robins, flycatchers and redstarts are regular and they can often be accompanied by the rarer warblers such as Yellow-browed, Barred or Icterine. Hauxley and Druridge Bay are genuine 'hotspots' with many records of rarities.

Firecrest

Winter: December through to march is the time to look for sea-duck, 'sawbills' and divers. Red-throated Diver (below) lack their red throats in winter and can appear white with dark upper parts. They are common along the Northumberland coast in winter and are often seen very close inshore. Look for their 'upturned' tilted head attitude and red eye.

Red-throated diver (winter)

Goldeneye, Long-tailed Duck, Scaup and Common Scoter often winter around the Coquet estuary with large flocks of both Lapwing and Golden Plover, and smaller groups of Dunlin, Redshank and Bar-tailed Godwit. Whilst a walk along the 'old harbour' may well produce Little Egret (a new arrival in 2000 and now well established), Brent Goose, Jack Snipe, Peregrine and Twite (sometimes 30+) along with flocks of both Wigeon and Teal feeding on the grasses and margins of the marsh. The visitor should also find Stonechat and possibly Snow or Lapland bunting. Short-eared and Barn owls can be seen in most years.

The beach at Warkworth has regular flocks of Sanderling and the harbour at Amble may hold Glaucous and Mediterranean Gull as well as Eider, Cormorant and Turnstone. Hauxley and Druridge Bay Country Park are favoured sites of the Smew, both 'redheads' and the striking black and white 'winter nun'. These birds often commute between several sites along Druridge Bay, a winter home to herds

Snow bunting

of Whooper Swan. By contrast, with the exception of Caistron, another good wildfowl reserve, the Coquet can seem devoid of birds at this time of the year, especially the woodlands and high ground, but the more persistent birder may find Crossbill and Siskin in the conifer forests, whilst moorland edges may produce Black Grouse or even Hen Harrier.

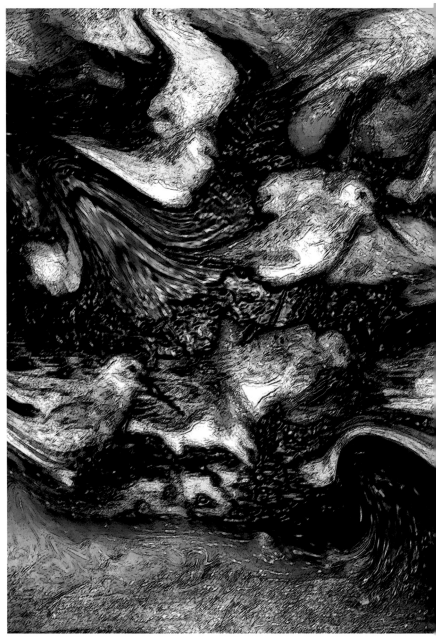

An abstract mixed media study of Dunlin painted by the author in 2019. This picture was produced as one of a series of artworks looking to capture movement. The author is a particular enthusiast of kinetics and 'Op art'.

St Oswald's Way

'St Oswald's Way is a long-distance walking route, exploring some of the finest landscapes and fascinating history of Northumberland. The route links some of the places associated with St Oswald, the King of Northumbria in the early 7th century, who played a major part in bringing Christianity to his people.

From Holy Island (Lindisfarne) in the north, St Oswald's Way follows the stunning Northumberland coast, before heading inland across beautiful countryside to Heavenfield and Hadrian's Wall in the south, a distance of 97 miles (156 km). You will find castles, coastline, islands, scenic river valleys, hills, attractive villages, forest and farmland on your walk.'
From the official website www.stoswaldsway.com

St Oswald's Way Walking Route is divided into six sections from north to south:

1. Holy Island to Bamburgh 19 miles / 31 km
2. Bamburgh to Craster 14 miles / 22 km
3. Craster to Warkworth 13.5 miles / 21.5 km
4. Warkworth to Rothbury 18 miles / 29 km
5. Rothbury to Kirkwhelpington 15 miles / 24 km
6. Kirkwhelpington to Heavenfield 17.5 miles / 28.5 km

Warkworth to Rothbury 18 miles / 29 km

From the village of Warkworth (page 82) St Oswald's Way meanders along the Coquet valley until it reaches the villages of West Thirston and Felton. It's a good place to stop and break the journey. The medieval bridge here is pedestrianised and offers an excellent view over the river. This is probably the most reliable spot along the river to see Kingfisher.

This stretch of the walk can often produce soaring Common Buzzard (right) and visitors should check the hedgerows for Long-tailed Tit, Tree Sparrow and Bullfinch.

St Oswald's Way after passing through the delightful villages of West Thirston and Felton, heading west towards Rothbury.

The route from Warkworth to Rothbury is the second longest section of the St Oswald's Way, a distance of 18 miles / 29 km. For the visiting birdwatcher I would suggest that the section between Felton and Warkworth is rather less scenic and unproductive, passing through areas of farmland and therefore unlikely to add any sightings of species that can't be seen further west.

The landscape (mainly given over to sheep farming) west of Felton becomes topographically and scenically much more interesting making Felton an ideal place to base oneself. There are bed and breakfasts and The Northumberland Arms Hotel offering accommodation and fine food. There is also a fine cafe named 'The Running Fox' serving, meals and afternoon teas.

The walk passes Felton Park through woodland overlooking the river, under the A1 and along riverside paths to Weldon Bridge (pictured page 30).
The route then stays on the southern side of the Coquet, glimpsing the historic Brinkburn Priory on the other side of the river, through attractive rolling farmland to Rothbury, 'the Capital of Coquetdale', before heading south-west to Simonside (page 70).

Dipper are present along the entire length of the Coquet west from Felton, where they can normally be spotted below the bridge. This pastel study was produced by the author in 1996.

A winter study of a Kestrel at Weldon Bridge with The Anglers Arms in the background. 30 *Pastel by the author 1994.*

Upper Coquetdale

'Between Shillmoor and Windyhaugh, a distance of three miles, the eye has little to rest on except the rounded contour of the grassy hills or the flashing runnels of the stream'

W W Tomlinson, *Comprehensive Guide to The County of Northumberland*, 1888

The area of hill country known as Upper Coquetdale, lies on the north-western edge of Northumberland and forms the border at the Cheviot hills with Scotland. The Cheviots, although volcanic in origin, appear today as rounded in their outline and, other than the highest peaks which are heather covered, they are steep sided, grassy and are grazed by sheep and cattle.

This area lies within the Northumberland National Park, the River Coquet dividing the Otterburn training area into two halves. The southern section is used for live firing by the army and is closed to the public on at least 300 days of the year and only open on some bank holidays, over Christmas and during the lambing season. Arrangements for public access are explained in a leaflet available from tourist information centres or the National Park Authority. This area is probably the best for Black Grouse, so bear this information in mind if this species is the one you would most like to see.

The northern section, bounded approximately by the route of the old drove road known as Clennel Street, has access at all times and it is here that most of the higher ground is found, rising to over 619 metres on Windy Gyle, with several peaks over 500 metres: 'Beefstrand' 516 metres; 'Blackbraes' 506 metres; and 'Shillhope Law' 510 metres.

> *First Philhope-burn (his next and near akin,*
> *As sprung from Thirlemore) to his aid came in,*
> *Then Buckhams-Walls, Blind-burn, and Carles-croft streams,*
> *Pour'd in their forces - 'gather'd from th' extremes*
> *Of English ground' : - next Rohope's friendly flood*
> *Joined them at Slime-foot by a winding road,*
> *From Rohope's Fells - from whence he takes his name.*
> *And from whose scarry sides his birth does claim.*
> *Next Barrough-burn, whose waters many a mile*

Poem about the tributaries of the Upper Coquet, taken from Upper Coquet-dale its history, traditions, folk-lore and scenery (1903), David Dippie Dixon.

Upland Plateau

The upland plateau volcanic lavas of the old red sandstone period is gouged by several fast-flowing burns such as the Alwin and Usway, tributaries of the Coquet, which itself rise further west at Brownhart Law. From here the Pennine Way meets with an unclassified road that criss-crosses the river, closely hemmed in by massive steep-sided hills rising straight from the river bed. From Makedon to the spectacular gorge at Barrow Scar, a distance of some 10 miles, the river twists and turns before emerging out into a broad flood plain at Alwinton.

To the south of the Cheviots the character of the Upper Coquet changes, rounded volcanic hills give way to the irregular topography of the cementstones and fell sandstone outcrops of 'Door Hill' (415 metres), 'Barrow Scar' (244 metres), Harbottle Craggs (335 metres) and Yearning Crags (244 metres). These rocky outcrops punctuate the wet acid peaty soil with a predominant vegetation of heather, occasional birch and bilberry. The main exposed crags are found along the Alwin valley. Diversity of habitat exists with a number of relict woodlands, with birch the commonest tree although oak, ash and alder are all well-represented along with the many coniferous plantations. One delightful walk in this region takes in one of these coniferous forests at Kidland (NT910120) and follows the route of Clennel Street, probably the best known of all the border 'streets' or crossings between Scotland and England.

Ring Ouzel.

It takes its name from the deserted village of Clennel and is a wonderful pathway used by walkers heading from Alwinton to the Cheviots. It was once a prehistoric trade route linking the Northumbrian outposts of the Votadini with tribal territories in the north. Later it was used by medieval monks, border reivers, drovers and smugglers, indeed the remoteness of the area made it a popular place for illicit whisky stills, one of them 'Rory's Still' was still in use in the 19th century. Present day visitors can take refreshments in Alwinton's inn, The Rose and Thistle (Sir Walter Scott once stayed here), its name suggestive of an allegiance to both England and Scotland.

Alwinton village.

Wild primrose.

The Birds

Upland breeding cycles are short and dependent on weather conditions. For other than early nesting species, such as Dipper, Mistle Thrush and Crossbill, most arrive and begin their display and breeding from April onwards, often after the last snows of winter have disappeared. At this time of the year curlew and Lapwing return to the moors and are joined by the forerunner of the summer visitors, the Ring Ouzel, which nests among the rocky screes and fell sandstone outcrops. On higher ground, the plaintive whistle of the Golden Plover can be heard together with the many Meadow Pipits and musical Skylark. Late April and early May see Dippers searching the sparkling fast flowing burns for the abundance of stonefly and mayfly to feed their young, which by now have often fledged just as Common Sandpiper, Oystercatcher and Redshank set up their breeding territories. On the heathery slopes Red Grouse sound their 'go-back', 'go-back', 'go-back', call as they fly low over the moors. Spring and early summer are without doubt the best times to visit Upper Coquetdale, with both migrant and resident birds at their most visible.

Whinchat.

It is not necessary to walk miles to encounter the moorland specialities, as most can be seen from the car or by picking a good high vantage point and scanning the moors with binoculars or better still a telescope. This method is more likely to disclose any birds of prey or even Raven. Merlin are best looked for on the ground as they will often sit for hours on vantage points such as a boulder or tuft of heather. Other raptors such as Sparrowhawk, Kestrel or even a Golden Eagle will often rise hundreds of feet on warm thermals and this is where a telescope is a must. That dot several 'miles' up, will no doubt be a bird of prey!

At the small farmsteads with isolated shelter belts of mature trees, the visitor should be on the lookout for Spotted Flycatcher and Tree Pipit. Swallow, House martin and Swift patrol the skies above the farm buildings and one should check telegraph wires for the 'banana shape' of a perching Cuckoo especially watchful around areas of heather, bracken and rough grassland, home to donor species such as Meadow Pipit and Whinchat.

Another important area for birds in this sparse landscape, are dry stone walls, as they are a favourite breeding location for Wheatear and wagtails. By June-July the breeding cycle is coming to an end and identification skills can be stretched to the limit, with families of Willow Warbler, Whinchat and other juvenile birds everywhere. Oystercatcher and Redshank start to move downstream and by August the moors can seem deserted. For the visitor a trip to either Caistron or the coast may well be more rewarding, however, cooler weather usually means better walking conditions and for the more persistent birder, the onset of winter months may well produce a wandering Hen Harrier or even Golden Eagle as immature birds of this species have been seen on more than one occasion.

Timings

All year:
Heron, Mallard, Sparrowhawk, Buzzard, Goshawk, Kestrel, Red Grouse, possible Red Kite, Black Grouse, Grey Partridge, pheasant, Snipe, Stock Dove, Collared Dove, Dipper, Long-eared Owl, Goldcrest, Siskin, Coal Tit, Redpoll, Reed Bunting, Grey and Pied Wagtail, Raven.

Spring and early summer: Teal, Goosander, Merlin, Quail, Oystercatcher, Golden Plover, Lapwing, Curlew, Redshank, Common Sandpiper, Sand Martin, Swallow, House Martin, Swift, Tree Pipit, Whinchat, Cuckoo, Wheatear, Ring Ouzel, Spotted Flycatcher.
June records for Turtle Dove and Golden Oriole.

Late autumn and winter; Hen Harrier, Fieldfare, Redwing, finch flocks, which may include Brambling, possible Twite and Snow Bunting.

Hen Harrier.

Barrowburn Hay Meadows SSSI

The ancient upland hay meadows of the Northumberland National Park are internationally rare and those at Barrowburn are some of the best in Europe. Hay meadows were once a common sight in Coquetdale but sadly, as with other areas in the UK, they have all but disappeared. Indeed over 97% of British hay meadows have vanished since the Second World War. The flowers present in these rare habitats can be traced back to ancient Britain as the Domesday book records hay meadows in 8 out of 10 settlements. The Corncrake is another of Coquetdale's extinct species once described as common up until the 1950s it could be found throughout the Coquet valley and into upper Coquetdale, its rasping monotonous call could being heard on many summer evenings.

The meadows at Barrowburn lie in one of the prettiest locations in the Cheviots and support many plants typically found in northern hay meadows. These include meadow buttercup, wood crane's bill, pignut, bitter vetch, rough and autumn hawkbit, cat's ear, selfheal, common bird's foot trefoil, yellow rattle and oxeye daisy. It is a sobering experience to listen to the buzz of the thousands of insects, pipits and Skylarks that depend on this habitat and compare it to our lowland lifeless monocultures. Best time to visit: June and July

The once common Corncrake was driven out of Coquetdale by 'modern' farming practices. Hopefully it will return to Upper Coquetdale in the not too distant future. This pastel study by the author 1999.

Rare and Ancient Flowers in the Meadows

Wood crane's-bill   **Best time to see: June - July**
A characteristic plant of upland hay meadows. Its seed pods 'explode' when ripe, throwing the seeds away from the parent plant.

Yellow rattle   **Best time to see: May - Sept.**
A semi-parasitic flower, that feeds off nutrients in nearby grass roots. In doing so it helps restrict the vigorous grasses, allowing more delicate wildflowers to emerge. Its 'rattle' is from tiny seeds in their pods.

Pignut   **Best time to see: April - June**
With delicate, branched stems, and white umbels of small flowers. Shakespeare refers to pignut in The Tempest when Caliban says 'I pr'ythee, let me bring thee where crabs grow; And I with my long nails will dig thee pig-nuts; Show thee a jay's nest'

Eyebright   **Best time to see: June - September**
The eyebright is a beauty in miniature, with distinctive lobed petals and often, a bright yellow centre. So-called because it was traditionally used to treat eye infections.

Barrow Burn Wood

This small (3 hectare) ancient mixed deciduous woodland is a SSSI and consists of a mixture of alder, hazel and willow. Owned by The Northumberland Wildlife Trust and accessed via the footpath that leads from just south of Alwinton Bridge to Barrow Scar. There are no formal paths on the reserve so care should be taken, as the terrain is very steep, uneven and quite often muddy.

Park at the parish church on the south side of the River Coquet and take the footpath that leads from Alwinton Bridge to Barrow Scar (2.5 km) OS Map reference NT 915 061. It is possible to incorporate this site into a circular walk that also allows for excellent views of the Cementstone layers of Barrow Scar (formed 350 million years ago) returning to Alwinton via the road at Linbriggs (approximately 8km).

Best visited in late April to June, birds including Sparrowhawk, Cuckoo, Treecreeper, Redstart, Pied Flycatcher and possibly Wood Warbler, although at the time of writing this species has seen a marked decline in numbers across Northumberland.

Badgers are present in the wood with otters using the stream. The site is managed in association with Defence Estates and Northumberland National Park Authority and features calcareous flushes including butterwort and marsh lousewort. The central part of the site has a ground flora of ramsons (wild garlic) and wild primrose, with some opposite-leaved golden saxifrage.

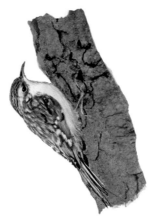

Tree Creeper.

Further exploration of these beautiful uplands is possible by checking out access information with The National Park and the MOD as walking is restricted when there are live firing sessions. This area known as the Otterburn ranges covers some 90 square miles and is one of the most remote landscapes in the United Kingdom. The limited visitor access has meant birdlife has flourished. Linshiels lake, approximately 1km south of the hamlet of Linbriggs, and Ramsey's Burn, another 1km further, are amongst several productive areas with Merlin, Buzzard, Lapwing, Curlew, Skylark, Raven and possible Black Grouse.

Looking East towards Harbottle Castle and village.

Harbottle Crags and Lough

Above a sharp bend in the Coquet known as 'The Devils Elbow' and lying in a hollow of heather covered hills, are the grey-brown stone cottages of Harbottle, at one time one of the most important military outposts of England. The first castle was built in 1160 by the combined efforts of Henry II and the Bishop of Durham and was to house the principal garrison of the Middle March for centuries. Destroyed by the Scots, re-built stronger, besieged again, only this time without success, it was, in 1515 (as the official residence of the keeper of Redesdale), to receive Margaret Tudor, Countess of Angus, the widow of James IV of Scotland and sister to Henry VIII. Here she gave birth to a daughter, another Margaret, whose grandson was to become James I of England, so ending centuries of feuding between the two peoples.

Crossbill.

In the 17th century the castle finally fell into ruin and many of its stones were used for the 'new' Harbottle Castle, a dignified house to the east of the village, which has two rows of stone houses, a church and a pub, The Star Inn. Throughout the Second World War there was a Royal Observer Corps post on the hilltop amongst the ruins of Harbottle Castle. One observer, T Logan, wrote in *Clippings of Upper Coquetdale*: 'On a quiet moonlight night, I was struck by the thought that we were only the latest in a long line of watchers who had stood on guard, more or less in the same spot over the centuries since the castle was built, but we were the first to be looking for an attacker in the sky!'

There is a theory that the term 'Jizz' or 'Giss' used for the general impression, shape and size of a bird came from the charts used by the Observer Corps for recognising German aircraft during the Second World War, however it proceeds the war era and was first used in the 1922 publication *Bird Haunts and Nature Memories* by Thomas Coward.

On the peel's farm, a field called 'Wolver's Law' reputedly marks the southern boundary of the ancient Selby's Forest which stretched from the Coquet to the top of Cheviot. Legend has it that the last wolf in Coquetdale was killed here, hence the field name.

This beautiful reserve lies half a mile (0.8km) west of the village of Harbottle, on the road to Alwinton, and is accessed via the forestry commission car park. The habitat here is varied and so, accordingly, are the birds. Best visited in spring (late April) and early summer, the mixed woodland by the roadside will often have Great Spotted Woodpecker. Other birds to look for include Redstart, Blackcap, Garden Warbler, Long-tailed Tit and Treecreeper.

The River Coquet runs close to the road at this point and holds many of the same riverine species as Upper Coquetdale with Dipper, Grey and Pied Wagtail much in evidence. Goosander are common on this stretch of the river and it was here in 1941 that the first breeding record for England was established. Look out for Bullfinch, Redpoll, Marsh and Coal Tit as well as Siskin. There is also a good chance of Spotted Flycatcher (late May onwards) - dead projecting branches are a favourite perching site.

Siskin.

Tree Pipit.

From the car park a signposted track leads up to Harbottle Hill crowned by the 27ft-high Drake Stone or (draag stone), said to be a relic of the druids and formerly used for worship. The stone was also thought to possess healing powers and sick children were passed over it in the belief that a cure was possible. In spring Common Cuckoo, Meadow Pipit, Tree Pipit and Common Crossbill should all be present with Roding Woodcock at dusk. The entire reserve is dominated by heather and bracken punctuated by craggy outcrops of fell sandstone and waterlogged mires supporting typical mire species such as common cotton grass, hares tail cotton grass, deer grass, cranberry, round leaved sundew and bog asphodel. Bilberry, crowberry, and bog myrtle (scarce in Northumberland) complete the mix. Remnants of high-level woodland exists with plant species such as chickweed wintergreen and climbing covydales. Continue on the path, which eventually arrives at the Drake Stone set amongst other rocky areas, offering a fine view of the village of Harbottle below and the rest of Coquetdale stretching eastwards. Tiger beetles can often be found on the sandy paths along with adder, slow worm and common lizard. Also look out for the impressive male emperor moth, a fluffy, grey-brown species with big peacock-like eyespots on all four wings and pinky-red markings at the wingtips. It is the only large moth with eyespots on all four wings and, unlike the female, can often be seen during the day. Butterflies present include the large heath and green hairstreak.

A path leads up to the Drake Stone and Lough.

Harbottle Lough

The acidic, nutrient deficient soils on the higher parts of the reserve support cotton grass whilst the wetter areas are sphagnum covered. Regular burning maintains the typical heather cover for Red Grouse, the moor's only permanent resident, which will readily burrow through snow to search out its normal food of bilberry and other low growing plants. As with Upper Coquetdale, when the snow has melted and new herbage starts to emerge, birds such as Skylark return to breed. They can be seen on the lower slopes, with Reed Bunting, Meadow Pipit and Pheasant. Ring Ouzel prefer the higher ground and can be seen from the track leading to Harbottle Lough (pictured) which, although unspectacular, has a record (amongst others) for Great-grey Shrike and Grey Phalarope in full summer breeding plumage.

Great Grey Shrike.

The pebbly grit at Millstone edge near the Lough was formerly used for sharpening scythes. Folklore has it that workmen sent to drain the lough were 'much alarmed and forthwith fled on hearing the following warning uttered in sepulchral tones, issuing from the depths of the dark mountain tarn:

> 'Let alone: let alone !
> or a'll droon Harbottle,
> an the peels
> an the bonny Holystone.'

The army's red flag, which normally flies near the gate, does not apply to the reserve, but do not pass the MoD signs at the reserve boundary. A public footpath runs from the Forestry Commission car park through the northern edge of the reserve as far as the MoD firing range, and then northwards leaving the reserve and entering West Wood for a round trip back to the car park.

Timings

All year: Grey Heron, Sparrowhawk, Kestrel, buzzard, possible Goshawk, Red Grouse, Pheasant, Long-eared Owl, Tawny Owl, Great Spotted and Green Woodpecker, Dipper, Pied and Grey Wagtail, Crossbill, Bullfinch, Siskin, Coal Tit, Redpoll.

Spring-summer: Ring Ouzel, Wheatear, Curlew, Nightjar, Merlin, Goosander, Raven, Whinchat, Wood Warbler (scarce), Short-eared Owl, Spotted Flycatcher, hirrundines.

Late autumn-winter: Mixed tit flocks, Hen Harrier, Fieldfare, Redwing, Brambling, record for Great Grey Shrike. The lough attracts water birds such as Teal, Goosander and Little Grebe, Canada Goose and Greylag Goose.

Access: Harbottle lies 9 miles (14.4 km) west of Rothbury. OS Map NT 922 040. Take B6341 and turn right on to an unclassified road after Hepple. Park in either the roadside car park for Harbottle castle or further along in the Forestry Commission car park. Dogs should be kept on a lead. Access at all times.

Holystone North Wood

The Amphibious Otter, now secure
on Coquet's peaceful shore
may roam at large, for Ned and Tug
will never harm him more
up Swindon Burn he may return
when salmon time comes on;
for poor old Ned in his cold bed
sleeps sound in Holystone.

Epitaph to eighteenth century eccentric Ned Allen, the weaver of Holystone, whose pastimes were spearing eels, fishing and hunting otter with his dog 'Tug-em', activities he found preferable to any work.

The quaint ancient village of Holystone is situated on the southern banks of the Coquet on the eastern margin of moorland running from Coquetdale to Redesdale. This 'debatable' land with its violent past still shows traces of ancient Britain, Roman occupation, Saxon settlements and relics of the middle ages.

The village is sheltered by Haremoor Law on its north side and by Holystone common to the south. For centuries the village and land lying south of the river was held by the Umfravilles of Harbottle Castle (now ruined), but after the dissolution of the monasteries, Holystone passed into the hands of various owners. Visitors to Holystone's two reserves may like to see the Lady's Well, owned by the National Trust and set amongst trees. The well is a quadrangle basin (given a rim of masonry in 1780) within a neatly kept enclosure. At one time a key for its gate had to be obtained from the Salmon Inn (now sadly closed), so the site is open at all times. A stone statue from Alnwick Castle once stood in the centre of the well, but this was removed and placed at the west end of the pool and substituted by a stone cross bearing the inscription

In this place
PavlinVs the bishop
baptized
three thovsand northvmbrians
Easter DC XXV11

Jay at Holystone North Wood painted by the author in 2018.

The well is situated 300 yards behind what used to be The Salmon Inn, which dates from the 16th century. It has oak beams and the listed open fireplace hides a priest hole used as a hiding place for monks during the persecutions of the same period.

Holystone consists of two reserves about 1km apart, which together provide marvellous examples of both upland and moorland edge valley woodland. First impressions from the forestry commission car park suggest large expanses of coniferous plantations, but these areas only serve to hide a beautiful upland sessile oak wood carpeted by bracken, wood-sorrel and mosses such as Leucobryun glaucum, containing the uncommon chickweed wintergreen.

Nightjar.

The upland oak wood's carpet of brackens and other cover provides the right habitat for ground nesting birds such as Pheasant, Woodcock and the rarer Nightjar. The latter two species will be almost impossible to see during the day and should be looked for at dusk. The Woodcock patrols the sky in a regular pattern above its breeding territory, calling frequently. The Nightjar's strange churring can be heard throughout the night, normally starting 15 minutes before sunset. As darkness falls over the woods listen for the low ioo-oo-ooi of the Long-eared Owl, sounding more like a moan than the more familiar hoot of the Tawny Owl.

The abundance of moribund trees, dead branches, holes and loose bark provides a variety of nesting sites for tits and woodpeckers which are joined in spring by visitors from Africa like the Redstart, Tree pipit and Pied Flycatcher.

Another summer visitor, the Wood Warbler, although choosing to nest on the ground will often be heard singing from the upper canopy of the wood. Listen for their beautiful metallic song, like the sound of a spinning coin coming to rest. Coal Tit and Chaffinch are by far the most abundant species in the coniferous woods, but the visitor should expect Siskin, Bullfinch and, in good cone years, Crossbill.

Spring day at Yardhope.

Holystone Burn

The small silvery burns have banks of alder, ash and willow, the valley woods being a mixture of wych elm, oak and birch with aspen on the valley floor. The understory has probably the finest show of juniper in the county attracting specialities such as the juniper pug moth. Amongst the hazel, hawthorn and willow, the visitor should also find primrose, dog's mercury and red campion. Wet drain areas from moorland have common reed in dense stands, their even size and age suggesting they may have been planted, probably in the 18th century. The woodland edge is marked mainly by crowberry and bilberry, fringed by bog myrtle, marsh lousewort, marsh violet, common butterwort, lesser twyblade and broad-leaved cottongrass.

In spring look for the dapper Pied Flycatcher in both the north wood and Yardhope Oaks.

At the North Yardhope (west side) of the reserve, upstream of the forestry car park, at roughly 3km, the broadleaved woods extend up the north slopes of the valley into an area known as the Yardhope Oaks, an area of sessile oak woodland at an unusually high altitude (circa 200m), on dry, steep slopes above Holystone burn. The reserve is managed by the Northumberland Wildlife Trust in partnership with the Forestry Commission, with the conifers being slowly removed to allow natural woodland to re-establish itself. A footpath allows visitors access to this area via the eastern section of the woodland, where juniper is an important component and there is juniper scrub for about 1000m either side of the burn.

Juniper scrub occurs at only three sites in Northumberland: the Coquet valley here at Holystone, Allendale district and around Cheviot. At Holystone Common, look for areas of bog myrtle with purple moor grass, a particular feature of the uplands of this part of Coquetdale.

Holystone Common.

Two locally important ferns have been recorded on the south bank of the stream in the oaks area - oak fern and beech fern. Two other important species have been recorded on the site - lesser twayblade and the rare cotton grass. Roe deer are present in good numbers and any trees planted on the site need to be protected from deer browsing. Other species recorded are badger and red squirrel. Bird species known to breed on the site include Pied Flycatcher, Merlin, Green Woodpecker, Greater Spotted Woodpecker, Dipper, Goosander and Common Sandpiper. The site has two species of reptile - adder and common lizard, and two amphibians - common frog and common toad. The northern wood ant occurs in the reserve: this is a very local species in North East England. The juniper pug moth has been seen in large numbers. In total, 186 species of moths and butterflies have been recorded on this site.

Redstart.

The Birds

The adjoining moorlands have the usual upland birds found in this and other parts of Upper Coquetdale. Red Grouse are numerous, together with Curlew and Whinchat. Patient scanning of moors may well reveal Merlin and perhaps Peregrine. Black Grouse frequent these moors but do not be tempted to cross the range boundary - large expanses of the moor are visible without the need to do so. If you are looking for Black Grouse in particular, check with the Northumberland National Park office in Rothbury for access details.

Timings

All year: Heron, Woodcock, Sparrowhawk, Buzzard, Great Spotted Woodpecker, Green Woodpecker, Long-eared Owl, Tawny Owl, Dipper, Kingfisher, (river), Grey Wagtail, Jay, Bullfinch, Pied Wagtail, Coal Tit, Chaffinch, corvids, thrushes, Goldcrest, Red Grouse, Tree Creeper.

Spring-summer: Wood Warbler, Redstart, Pied Flycatcher (Yardhope Oaks or north wood), Chiff-chaff, Willow Warbler (common). Spotted Flycatcher (village/Lady's Well area).

Late May onwards: Grey Wagtail, Dipper and Goosander (river), Merlin, Peregrine, Curlew, Blackcap, Whitethroat, Nightjar, Whinchat.

Late autumn – winter: Mixed tit flocks, corvids, Fieldfare, Redwing, possible wandering raptors including Hen Harrier.

Access: Situated half a mile (0.8km) west of Holystone Village. Park in the Forestry Commission car park. An information board shows a number of circular walks marked by coloured posts. For Holystone Burn, continue (on foot) on the tarmac road a short distance up the hill and across the cattle grid.

Holystone Common.

Grasslees Burn Wood

Grasslees Burn is a small tributary of the Coquet entering the river between Hepple and Holystone and its 8km course roughly follows the B6341 from the direction of the village of Elsdon. Use the parking lay-by for the Darden Lough walk, about 0.5 miles north of Grasslees Farm (nearest postcode NE65 7AU, grid ref OL42 NY958982) on the B6341, where there is space for several cars. This small but ornitholgically interesting reserve is best combined with a walk for the physically fit to Darden Lough (page 62).

To reach the Northumberland Wildlife Trust reserve of Grasslees Burn Wood, visitors should follow the Darden Lough walk a short distance to the valley floor until it crosses the burn but bear right on the marked route on the north side of the burn without crossing the bridge at this point. At the time of writing (2020) the reserve access is rather unclear as the marker posts have become faded.

The public footpath from the lay-by to the reserve is uneven and unsurfaced, very muddy in places and there is a small, narrow footbridge in the valley bottom (use this bridge to explore the open lower moorland areas as they can be productive for other species not found in the reserve). Access is via a small footbridge and two fences without stiles. There are moderately steep slopes in places, and the terrain is very muddy and often wet in the valley bottom. There are no footpaths within the reserve, and tussocky/stony ground has to be negotiated.

Willow Warbler. In spring and summer listen for the its beautiful plaintive descending song often delivered from the top of a birch tree.

Common Redstart painted by the author in 1999.

The reserve occupies of an area of sloping ground with ancient semi-natural woodland containing stands of alder and birch in the wetter areas, with oak, rowan and ash where the ground is drier. At the northern (burn) end of the site are butterwort, lousewort and marsh violet.

Nearer the burn there are fens dominated by yellow flag and meadowsweet. Parts of the site are bracken-dominated but contain a good spring flora. Spring/summer birds include Pied Flycatcher, Redstart, Wood Warbler, Cuckoo, Willow Warbler and other common upland woodland birds including Woodcock. Roe deer are now excluded to encourage regeneration of parts of the woodland, which seems to be successful, particularly for birch. The reserve is managed by the Northumberland Wildlife Trust in association with the Defence Estates of Northumberland National Park Authority.

Grasslees Burn with tinder fungus growing from a dead silver birch. Trees here are mostly alder, which were once coppiced for charcoal for use in the local iron industry.

Darden Lough and Moorland Walk

Around 350 million years ago a shallow tropical sea washed against the bare volcanic hills of the Cheviot. Massive river deltas fed into it, pushing great fans of silts and sands westwards. These compressed into the rocks of the Carboniferous period about 290 to 354 million years ago that form the crags and hills we see today. The rocky outcrops of fell sandstone that are visible on this walk were once sands swept along by the currents of these ancient rivers.

Merlin (male).

The lower slopes of this walk were once covered in blanket forestry but the landscape was cleared allowing heather moorland to re-establish. In August a stunning purple carpet makes for a delightful walk and although it is not necessary to climb all the way to the lough (a 4.5 mile circular route) to witness the varied bird species, the views become increasingly spectacular the higher one ventures, with almost 360-degree panoramic vista of the surrounding hills including the Otterburn rages and Cheviot in the north, Kielder to the west and Coquetdale to the east.

Reaching Cloven Crag there are fine views towards Key Heaugh and Darden Parlour and visitors may find that this is a good a spot as any to sit and survey the surrounding moorland. In spring and early summer there are the constant calls of Meadow Pipit, Skylark, Cuckoo and Red Grouse with their characteristic 'go back, go back, go back' call. These are all species that can be found along the 'Simonsides'.

Ring Ouzel at Darden Lough painted by the author 2018.

Darden Lough at a height of 374 metres.

As with most birdwatching it is always more productive to find a comfortable place to sit rather than walk for miles. Moorland can seem devoid of birds so careful scanning of the skyline, ridges and crags will always be the best option. Despite the male Ring Ouzel's striking black and white appearance the 'mountain blackbird' can be incredibly hard to see but prefers screes, crags and rocky areas and, as with other species, it's a major advantage if one is familiar with their song. Likewise Wheatear, Raven and Peregrine prefer rocky habitats so please do not be tempted to walk to close to them.

Merlin will often sit in one place for hours on a good vantage point, either a tuft of mature heather or a rock, so it is well worth scouring the landscape with binoculars but a telescope would be better still. Also worth noting is the direction of the wind. Just as aircraft take off into the prevailing wind, birds of prey will do likewise and buzzard will often be found hanging in the air above a ridge where they receive the maximum lift.

Red Grouse are numerous here, but fly extremely quickly, often just above ground level. Observers will need to be alert to catch them as their plumage is well matched by the heather landscape. Unlike the Skylarks, Pipits and other species mentioned above, Red Grouse are present on these heather moorlands all year but for the best chance of seeing any of the above I would recommend a visit in late April/May. The heather is, however, at its most colourful in August.

Check fence posts and rocky areas for Wheatear.

Caistron

A mile (1.6km) from the village of Hepple and four miles (6.4km) west of Rothbury is Caistron, a series of lakes lying next to the River Coquet, formed by the extraction of gravel from the river itself. This activity ceased in 1969 when planning permission was granted to extract from the adjacent fields. The resultant wet pits have been restored into a nature reserve which can boast records for over 180 species including Great Reed Warbler, Black-necked Grebe and ferruginous duck to name a few. Consisting of a series of pools, reedbeds, wader scrapes and shingle areas, the reserve has been landscaped using a variety of restoration techniques. Alder, willow and conifers have been planted, complementing the many trees that existed before extraction commenced.

Caistron is worth a visit at any time of the year with over 75 breeding species, a wealth of spring and autumn passage visitors and many wintering species such as white-fronted geese, pintail and smew.

The variety and numbers of species attracted to Caistron is no accident. The extraction company have used many of the tried and tested methods employed at other man-made reserves throughout Britain. For example, small stands of mature trees were circumnavigated during extraction of the gravel beds. This effectively left them standing as islands when the land flooded; the isolation providing many ready-made breeding habitats for wildfowl such as Mute Swan, Greylag Goose, Canada Goose, Shelduck, Teal, Mallard, Gadwall and Ruddy Duck. Other islands were created without tree cover, providing ideal habitat for large colonies (1500+) of Black-headed Gull to develop, together with a few pairs of Lesser Black-backed Gull. A bankside was constructed and this led to the arrival of a Sand Martin colony. Other fresh-water birds in evidence here are Moorhen, Coot, Goosander and Kingfisher.

Many bays and peninsulas have been formed to maximise the shingle shoreline, thus providing ideal habitat for breeding waders such as Oystercatcher, Ringed plover, Redshank and Common Sandpiper. Other breeding birds of note are Yellow Wagtail, Sedge, Grasshopper and Willow Warbler. The wooded and scrub areas have Redstart and Whitethroat with resident finches and tits. Arguably the most important feature of the reserve are its extensive shallow feeding areas for wading birds. They can reach impressive numbers with Spotted Redshank, Greenshank, Green and Wood Sandpiper all regular, while fish in the lakes can attract passing Osprey.

Timings

All year: Little Grebe, Heron, Mute Swan, Greylag Goose, Canada Goose, Wigeon, Teal, Mallard, Tufted Duck, Sparrowhawk, possible Goshawk, Kestrel, Red-legged Partridge, Grey partridge, Pheasant, Water Rail, Moorhen, Coot, Lapwing, Snipe, Black-headed Gull, Woodpigeon, Collared Dove, Tawny Owl, Kingfisher, Great-spotted Woodpecker, Skylark, Meadow Pipit, Grey Wagtail, Pied Wagtail, Dipper, thrushes, tits, Treecreeper, corvids, finches, Yellowhammer, Reed bunting.

Spring-summer: Great-crested Grebe, Cormorant, Shelduck, Gadwall, Shoveler, Pochard, Goosander, Osprey, Oystercatcher, Ringed Plover, Dunlin, Curlew, Redshank, Greenshank, Wood Sandpiper, Common Sandpiper, Black-headed Gull, Lesser Black-backed Gull, Herring Gull, Common Tern, Cuckoo, Swift, Sand martin, House Martin, Swallow, Yellow Wagtail, Redstart, Whinchat, Wheatear, Grasshopper Warbler, Sedge, Garden and Willow Warbler, Chiff-chaff, Spotted flycatcher.

Autumn-winter: Build up of post-breeding wildfowl, sometimes huge numbers. Hen Harrier, Peregrine and Merlin. Large concentrations of Lapwing and Golden Plover move downstream from upland breeding areas, joined by passage Ruff, Wood and Green Sandpiper, Curlew and Greenshank. Winter has records for Bittern, Pink-footed Goose, Bean and White-fronted Goose, Pintail, Smew, Water Pipit, Great Grey Shrike and Snow Bunting.

Other records include: Black Tern, Temminck's Stint, Turtle Dove, Wryneck, Black-necked Grebe, Great Reed Warbler, Hobby, Marsh Harrier, Whimbrel and Red-backed Shrike.

Access: Take the minor unclassified road 500m south of Hepple to Bickerton and Little Tosson. Park with care at Bickerton. There is a public footpath which allows for excellent views of the reserve.

Ringed Plover.

Caistron

Simonside Hills

Dominating the mid Coquet valley from whichever direction one approaches, stand the coarse fell sandstone hills of Simonside. Still retaining the distinct traces of glacial erosion, they provide spectacular views of not only Coquetdale but Tyneside, much of the Northumbrian coastline and the Cheviot hills to the west. Various peaks make up the range (from east to west): Gorley Pike (800ft), Lordenshaws hill (879ft), (here there are the remains of a British camp) Spy Law or 'The Beacon' (1,181ft), (the summit of which is capped by a cairn), Newton Peak (1,295ft) - then comes Simonside proper with its three peaks, Old Stell and Dove Crag (1,203ft), Simonside (1401ft), Tosson Peaks with its cliffs to the north (1,409ft), Tosson Hill and Ravens Heugh crags 1459ft, on the extreme west is Whitefield Hill (1,140ft) and finally, lower down, the green flat topped Tosson Burgh (746ft).

To the south of the Simonsides, bordering Harwood forest, is Selby's Cove, an opening in the rock where once lived the 'moss trooper' and notorious bandit Walter Selby. Legend also has it that the adjacent 'Croppies Hole' was the lair of a well-known fox without a tail (a cropped fox). He was said to have survived for many years by his superior cunning until he was run to death by a single huntsman and his pack of hounds on the sands of Amble, finally confused by the crashing waves of the North Sea.

Simonside's birds are similar to those of the upper Coquet and, as with most upland and conifer habitats, require patience. However these hills are still one of the best places for Ring Ouzel, Merlin and Peregrine, with Hen Harrier in winter. Breeding birds include the ubiquitous Meadow Pipit, Red Grouse, Golden Plover, Snipe, Curlew and possibly Dunlin and Short-eared Owl. Forest areas have breeding Sparrowhawk, Goldcrest and Mistle Thrush. Many walkers and climbers visit this area in midsummer so it is advisable to visit in the spring (Monday to Friday if possible) in the early morning or evening.

Goldcrest.

Abstract study titled 'The Fox of Croppies Hole'. This study is one of a series of multi-media 'kinetic' paintings from 2019 by the author.

Timings

All year: Sparrowhawk, Kestrel, Goshawk, Red grouse, Grey Partridge, Pheasant, Snipe, Woodcock, Woodpigeon, Stock Dove, Tawny Owl, Meadow Pipit, Wren, Dunnock, Robin, thrushes, Goldcrest, tits, Treecreeper, Jay, corvids, Linnet, Redpoll, Crossbill.

Spring-summer: Merlin, Peregrine, Golden Plover, Cuckoo, Tree Pipit, Redstart, Wheatear, Ring Ouzel, Willow Warbler, Chiff-chaff.

Winter: Possible Hen Harrier, Golden Eagle has been sighted on more than one occasion.

Access: 3 miles (4.8km) south of Rothbury on the B6342 Scots Gap/Wallington road. Turn right onto an unclassified road signposted Simonside. Carry on past the first car park on the right until you reach the Forestry car park set among the trees. Here an information board details several circular walks. The Red trail takes around two to three hours to complete and is the only one that leads to the moorland and peaks. It entails a steady climb through coniferous woodland (half an hour) before becoming steeper. A certain amount of fitness is required to climb to the top. Once here however, the views on a fine day are quite breathtaking. Add the sounds of Red Grouse, mewing Buzzard and the plaintive whistle of Golden Plover and the whole experience is quite memorable.

Golden Plover.

Grey Wagtail 'hawking' flies over Debdon Burn with Cragside House in the backgound. Mixed media by the author.

Cragside

Created by the first Lord Armstrong over a period of twenty years, Cragside's scenery and house are outstanding. A large stone mansion designed by London architect Richard Norman Shaw (the first house in the world to be lit by hydro-electricity) stands on a steep rocky hill, which is terraced with many walks and accessed by a tarmac drive.

There are endless varieties of trees at Cragside and in June the whole estate is ablaze with colour from the many rhododendrons and azaleas. Huge boulders, remnants of the glacial period, lie among the woodland, showing visible marks of the ice age that may also be seen in the striated rocks above the house.

There are three freshwater lakes on the estate. Tumbleton, formed when the Debdon Burn was dammed, is the first to be visible as one enters the grounds. Next, in an anti-clockwise direction is the Blackburn lake. It has two hides and a car park. Nelly Moss lakes are the largest stretches of water and have picnic sites and parking facilities. Perhaps the most spectacular view is that from the dam at Tumbleton lake in the valley running towards the Coquet. Here the Debdon Burn is shaded by huge fir trees and with the iron bridge centrally positioned high above the winding path, combined with the distant elevated mansion house, a splendidly picturesque scene is created. There are some 40 miles of drives and footpaths, a National Trust shop, visitor centre and cafe. Even if your passion for birds outweighs any other, the house is not to be missed.

The birds

All year: Little Grebe, Heron, Mallard, Sparrowhawk, Kestrel, Pheasant, Moorhen, Coot, Woodcock, Tawny Owl, Long-eared Owl, Kingfisher, Green Woodpecker (now scarce), Great-spotted Woodpecker, Grey wagtail, Pied Wagtail, Dipper, tits including Marsh and Long-tailed, Nuthatch, Treecreeper, Jay, Siskin, Linnet, Pedpoll, Crossbill, Bullfinch, Goldcrest, Reed Bunting.

Spring-summer: Greylag Goose, Common Sandpiper, Cuckoo, Swift, Swallow, House martin, Sand martin, Tree Pipit, Redstart, Sedge Warbler, Whitethroat, Garden Warbler, Blackcap, Wood Warbler (now scarce), Spotted Flycatcher.
Autumn–winter: Fieldfare, Redwing, Brambling, occasional Waxwing. Records for White Stork, Bittern, Osprey, Hobby.

Weldon Bridge to Felton

This section of the river runs from The Angler's Arms, an ancient fishing hostelry and coaching inn at Weldon Bridge, to the picturesque village of Felton via Elyhaugh, Shothaugh and Felton Park. It is possible to walk the entire river course by using the St Oswald's Way, a distance of 6km. If walking from west to east start at the three-arched stone bridge dating from 1760, which replaced earlier bridges destroyed by flooding in 1744 and 1752, and pass under the newer road bridge. The mature deciduous woodland to the left has the usual woodland birds including Great-spotted Woodpecker and Tawny Owl.

Listen for the Great-spotted Woodpecker's alarm call, a repetitious 'keek keek keek', often delivered from the top of a tree.

The walk continues for some distance above the river valley and it is always worth scanning the skies for birds of prey such as Buzzard or a circling Sparrowhawk. At Elyhaugh the pathway passes closer to the river so Dipper, Goosander and Grey Wagtail should all be visible. This area is also very good spot for those lucky enough to see otter as they are often observed using the pool at Shothaugh on the south side of the river. This was once visible from the path but unfortunately it is now hidden by trees. As the walk crosses the Swarland Burn, the pathway climbs again and makes its way through delightful woodland, under the A1 and high above the Coquet gorge. This area and the subsequent parkland was created by Roger de Bertram of Mitford Castle in 1225 and has some fine specimen trees planted in Capability Brown fashion. The path ends at the stunning St Michael's church, Felton, built circa 1200.

Felton

The picturesque villages of Felton and West Thirston lie on the North and South sides of the River Coquet respectively, joined by two bridges of architectural note. The older, grade two listed, arched bridge is from the 15th century, while the newer Historic England listed concrete bridge was built in 1927 and used to carry the A1 traffic. The villages are now bypassed by the A1 and subsequently offer a peaceful and relaxing ambiance with some excellent walking and fishing. There is a splendid riverside picnic site, the legendary Running Fox artisan bakery, cafe and tea room, and a fine art gallery. The Northumberland Arms on the West Thirston side was built in the 1820s by Hugh Percy, 3rd Duke of Northumberland as a coaching inn.

The St Oswald's Way passes through the villages crossing the river. With the 'old bridge' pedestrianised it is possible to spend time here taking in the river views and it is probably the most accessible and reliable place on the entire river to see Kingfisher, grey wagtail and dipper, with possible Little Grebe, Goosander and occasionally Goldeneye in the winter months. There is a short circular walk through mixed woodland at Felton Park just to the north-west of St Michael's church, with all common woodland birds present. For a better chance of buzzard and other birds of prey, visitors should join the St Oswald's Way track towards the A1 underpass.

Grey Wagtail

From the riverside picnic area on the Felton side, take the short walk along the B6345, immediately turning left up an incline towards the beautiful grade 1 listed St Michael's church, built circa 1200 AD. The churchyard should not be overlooked and can be very productive during favourable conditions for migrants. From here the Felton Park circuit can be reached by taking the small tarmac road to the north and looking for a wooden sign on your right for 'Felton Fence'. Take this small track, keeping the tarmac road to your left and the track will rejoin it. The track runs along an elevated position overlooking some fine woodland, a regular place for Jay, which, despite being relatively common, can be extremely elusive. Listen for their loud screaming call. Alternatively heading west from the church, visitors can walk part of the St Oswald's Way across fine parkland to another splendid woodland, this time elevated above the Coquet.

The 15th century stone bridge looking west with West Thirston lying on the south side of the river.

Heading west along the St Oswald's Way through Felton Park. The path eventually passes through a gate into elevated woodland with fine views of the river below.

Heading from Mouldshaugh (Felton) to Acklington, the Coquet passes a delightful woodland known as the Groves, a good place to sit quietly and watch the river for otter.

Blackcap ♂

Nape grey with faint eye ring

Forehead and crown black

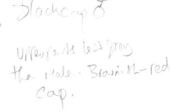

Blackcap ♀

Upperparts less grey than male. Brownish-red cap.

Male and female Blackcap. Common summer migrants to Northumberland, arriving in mid-April. Listen for the scratchy song of the male and the alarm call that resembles two stones being knocked together.

Sand martins are one of the first spring migrants to arrive on the Coquet, pictured here on a bend in the coquet below High Park Farm between Felton and Acklington.   *Mixed media study 2017.*

Felton to Warkworth

Leaving Felton on the West Thirston side of the bridge, a footpath follows the course of the river until it reaches High Park, where it climbs into farmland. The topography is rather unspectacular but sightings of Buzzard and Heron are regular and areas of rough grassland have been retained for breeding Skylark. In spring and summer there is a large active Sand Martin colony below High Park Farm and, as the path increases in height, there are lovely views over the river valley below.

The habitat on the next section of the St Oswald's Way to the unclassified road that leads from Acklington to the bridge at Brainshaugh, is of little ornithological interest as is the rest of the walk to Warkworth.

However, the river does offer far more pleasures if one detours from the St Oswald's Way to Brainshaugh where there are the remains of Brainshaugh Priory, which was established by Richard Tison around 1147 for Premonstratensian nuns and is grade 2 listed, the stunning Guyzance Hall and the beautiful Guyzance Weir.

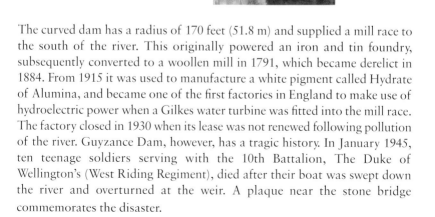

Areas of rough grassland have been preserved for the benefit of Skylark.

The curved dam has a radius of 170 feet (51.8 m) and supplied a mill race to the south of the river. This originally powered an iron and tin foundry, subsequently converted to a woollen mill in 1791, which became derelict in 1884. From 1915 it was used to manufacture a white pigment called Hydrate of Alumina, and became one of the first factories in England to make use of hydroelectric power when a Gilkes water turbine was fitted into the mill race. The factory closed in 1930 when its lease was not renewed following pollution of the river. Guyzance Dam, however, has a tragic history. In January 1945, ten teenage soldiers serving with the 10th Battalion, The Duke of Wellington's (West Riding Regiment), died after their boat was swept down the river and overturned at the weir. A plaque near the stone bridge commemorates the disaster.

Warkworth and the Coquet Estuary

Six miles (9.6km) south east of Alnwick lies the picturesque coastal village of Warkworth. Built in a classic defensive position inside a horseshoe of the River Coquet, its neck cut off by the castle, 'That worm-eaten hold of ragged stone' according to Shakespeare's Henry IV. The village retains its quiet elegance and old-world charm, despite the now considerable traffic that has increased in recent years.

From the birdwatcher's point of view, the variety of habitats and perhaps more importantly, its accessibility, makes this area one of the best in Northumberland with Hauxley and Druridge Bay only 3 miles away, Coquet Island 1 mile offshore and other good birding areas such as Craster and The Farne islands only half an hour's drive. There are essentially two main walks around Warkworth, but combined they will provide the visiting birdwatcher with a taste of all the habitats and subsequently the greater number of species.

Goldeneye can be found below the Norman bridge in winter.

The River Walk

Start your walk at the Norman bridge, which has a fortified gatehouse and was the only crossing point for traffic until 1965. Continue along the river bank past the Norman church of St Lawrence, which has its own detailed guide available. From here the footpath follows the river past a weir where Heron, Black-headed Gull and Mallard can usually be found. This spot will often have fishing Sandwich Tern from nearby Coquet Island (usually evening in summer), Goosander, Common Sandpiper, Redshank and Grey Wagtail. Winter brings Goldeneye and although usually found further downstream towards Amble, divers and grebes are not unknown. At the first bend in the river, below the castle, rowing boats can be hired in the summer (look for Pied and Grey Wagtail and bats in the summer). The woodland here has the usual species associated with this type of habitat - Sparrowhawk, Great-spotted Woodpecker, tits, Treecreeper, Blackcap, Garden Warbler, Robin. This is also a possible place to see red squirrel although they are declining because of the invasive greys. There is also an outside chance of seeing elusive otter on this stretch of the river, very early in the morning before dog walkers arrive.

✦ The 'Old harbour' and Estuary

The River Coquet once entered the sea further north than its present day position, until a great storm in 1765 forced the river to change its course. This left a series of islands, an un-navigable sand bar and Warkworth harbour silted up. Access to the sea became hazardous until, in 1836, a breakwater was built to change the river flow. Accordingly the town of Amble was born and by the following year, with the formation of the Warkworth Harbour Commission, a thriving port known as 'little Liverpool' was in operation. Coaling staithes were constructed and Amble built up a fine fleet of brigs, brigatines and schooners, all engaged in the coal trade with Scandinavia or London.

By the mid 1960s however, with the local mines defunct, ships requiring bigger, deeper ports and the closure of the National Coal Board staithes, the port's importance declined, leaving only the small fishing fleet. The estuary can be viewed from both the north and south sides of the river. The north side has the greater diversification of habitat but involves a good walk, viewing from the south can be done from the marina area and picnic site.

Short-eared Owl can be a regular sight in winter.

Walking to the old harbour, again start at the Norman bridge and cross the river. Head towards the cemetery and beach, up a steep tree-lined road with a football field to the right. Alternatively you can drive to the end of the road and the car park picnic site. Driving, however, misses out on the cemetery, which is a favoured spot for Tree Sparrow, Nuthatch and Bullfinch and possible migrants in the spring and autumn. Listen out for Grey Partridge along this road and common Whitethroat in spring/summer and it is not unusual to find Barn Owl here.

At the end of this lane (the car park has toilets), a gravel track leads straight down to the dunes with the golf course on the left and the 'old harbour' on the right. Climbing on to the highest dunes gives excellent views across the bay and any seabird movements are obvious. It's a good place to see terns and skuas in summer, fishing Gannets and in winter divers and grebes.

Take the track that passes through a large gate to the old harbour, estuary and north pier. This track skirts a large area of rough grassland punctuated by hawthorn and gorse and shallow lagoons excavated by English Nature. An area of reedbed lies between the track and the caravan park situated on higher ground. Skylark, Meadow Pipit and Stonechat are common here, and the area of reedbed is home to Reed Bunting and, in summer, Sedge and Grasshopper Warbler (listen for their constant 'reeling' sound, often delivered from any raised vegetation).

This saltmarsh is the third largest in Northumberland and is one of only five substantial areas on the coast of North-East England. North of the 'Castle Dike' is a small brackish lagoon, a lowland wetland with fen communities. This area has been 'opened up' by English Nature to allow for a further formation of the saltmarsh. The open tidal flats to the south of the dike form the main intertidal feeding area for waders and wildfowl within the Coquet estuary.

Stonechat.

Grasshopper Warbler.

Depending on the state of the tide, the section after the dike will have wading birds either very close or feeding on the muddy margins of the old water saltmarsh. With this in mind, as with all estuaries, a telescope would be an advantage. However the track here gives excellent views over the whole estuary with its sunken barges revealed at low water, one or two of them original Tyne keels of 'Weel may the keel row' fame. Waders here are dominated on a year-round basis by Redshank, but in winter they are outnumbered by Golden Plover (300+) with good numbers of Lapwing, Oystercatcher, Curlew, Turnstone and Ringed Plover, smaller numbers of Grey Plover, Bar-tailed Godwit, occasional Knot and Purple Sandpiper (north pier and staithes), while the beach area has Sanderling. Continue your walk to overlook the harbour area and look for Shelduck, Eider, Little Egret, Cormorant and gulls. Winter often brings white-winged gulls such as Iceland, and Glaucous, which is usually annual.

Timings

All year: Gannet (sea), Cormorant, Heron, Mute Swan, Wigeon, Teal, Mallard, Eider, Kestrel, Sparrowhawk, Grey Partridge, Pheasant, Oystercatcher, Ringed Plover, Dunlin, Snipe, Curlew, Redshank, Turnstone, Black-headed Gull, Herring Gull, Great Black-backed Gull, Guillemot, Puffin and Razorbill (sea), Woodpigeon, Skylark, Meadow Pipit, Pied Wagtail, Tree Sparrow (cemetery area), Stonechat.

Spring-summer: Lesser Black-backed Gull, Sandwich Tern, Roseate Tern (harbour), Arctic Tern, Little Tern (sea), Sand Martin, Yellow Wagtail, Wheatear, Grasshopper Warbler, Sedge Warbler.

Late autumn: Arrival of passage waders including Curlew Sandpiper, Whimbrel, Spotted Redshank and Greenshank.

July/Sept: Shearwater passage, Manx and possibly Sooty.

May/June - July/Oct: Passage migrants can include Black Redstart, Barred and Yellow-browed Warbler, Wryneck.

Winter: Divers and sea duck (sea), Scaup and grebes to the estuary. Regular Slavonian Grebe, Brent Goose, Peregrine (very regular), Jack Snipe, Short-eared Owl and Twite (often up to flocks of 30).

Rarities seen include White Pelican, Chilean Flamingo, Night Heron, Crane, Bee-eater, Hoopoe and Common Rosefinch.

✦ Coquet Island RSPB reserve

Approximately 1 mile (0.8km) from the mouth of the River Coquet at Amble, lies a small flat-topped island measuring around 16 acres surrounded by low sandstone cliffs and a broad rock platform at tide level. Coquet Island was purchased as Cockett Island in 1753 by the Duke of Northumberland from a certain John Widdrington together with 'all that Chappell within the said island being formerly parcel of the lords and possessions of the late dissolved monastery of Tynemouth'. The history of the island goes back to Saxon times, being the dawn of Christianity in Northern England. Bede speaks of 'the Eland of Cockett' as home to monks during the conversion of Northumbrians from barbarism to the light of faith.

By 1730 it was said to be uninhabited but in 1747 it had huts occupied by diggers of sea coal. Later, stone was quarried for repairs to the Duke of Northumberland's Syon House in Brentford. In 1823 a book of lithographs by Charlotte Florentia, third Duchess of Northumberland, described the island as 'containing about sixteen acres of land occupied chiefly as a rabbit warren although it is occasionally depastured by sheep'.

By the late 1800s the island became a popular resort for day trips, including steamboat trips that landed crowds from Tyneside. Once this became unfashionable the island once again was deserted apart from the lighthouse crew. By the middle of the twentieth century, keen naturalists could obtain visiting permits from the Duke's office or the Natural History Society of Northumberland, Durham and Newcastle upon Tyne. However, it soon became apparent that, because of disturbance from the ever-increasing use of small boats, Coquet Island was in desperate need of protection. In 1968 negotiations were started with various conservation bodies, culminating in the RSPB being granted a lease and it is now a protected bird reserve designated an SSSI.

The old Northumbrian name for a Puffin is a 'Tommy Noddy'.

Coquet Island viewed from Amble harbour

The peaty soil of the plateau gives support to a grassland dominated by Yorkshire-fug and Fescues, which is closely cropped by the island's rabbit population. Grazing resistant plants such as common ragwort and various species of dock are plentiful, giving cover to the many thousands of ground-nesting birds and although maritime plants such as thrift and sea campion have all but disappeared, there are dense stands of nettle providing the birds with additional cover. Seals can be viewed on the northern side of the island and dolphin sightings are regular.

Coquet Island presently supports internationally important numbers of breeding Sandwich Tern and the rarer Roseate Tern, with nationally important numbers of breeding Eider, Black-headed Gull, Common Tern, Arctic Tern and Puffin amongst countless other species. Although no landings are allowed on the island, the boat trip that circumnavigates during late spring and summer is well worthwhile. Approaching from the river mouth on a glorious summer's day soon reveals the island under a 'snowstorm' of gulls and terns and should not be missed. If, however, you do not get the chance of a visit, the waters between the mainland and the island can be viewed from the dunes on the minor road between Amble and Hauxley.

There is no public access or landing on Coquet Island because of the risk of disturbance to nesting birds, but boat trips sail from Amble harbour around the island.

Dolphins escorting a 'Puffin' cruise from Amble harbour to Coquet Island one mile offshore.

A wintry Coquet Island pastel by the author in 1999.

Timings

Winter: Divers (most commonly Red-throated), grebes, Cormorant, Eider, Long-tailed duck, Scaup, Scoter, Auks.

Spring/summer: Fulmar, passage Manx Shearwater, Shelduck, Ringed Plover, gulls, breeding Eider, Kittiwake, terns including the rare Roseate Tern, passage Gannet, Auks, Little Tern, passage migrants including rarities.

Autumn: Skuas including Pomarine, Arctic, Great and Long-tailed, Sooty Shearwater, Storm Petrel.

Rarities include Snow Goose, Ruddy Shelduck, Surf Scoter, Bridled Tern, Black Tern, Wryneck, Thrush Nightingale, Bluethroat, Savi's Warbler, Marsh Warbler, Scarlet Rosefinch and countless others.

Hauxley

The Northumberland Wildlife Trust reserve of Hauxley is essentially two fresh-water lagoons with islands, reed beds, 6 hides and a new information centre. Covering some 80 acres (32Ha), it lies 1.5 miles (2.4km) south of the town of Amble at the northern edge of Druridge Bay. Low Hauxley has been a bird ringing station for many years and it is from here that many of Northumberland's rarities have been recorded as its small private wood was one of the few natural features to remain untouched during the 1970s when much of this area was used for opencast mining operations.

As the mines became exhausted, large sections of Druridge Bay were re-landscaped and it is now a conservation area (including Cresswell Ponds) of around five miles (8km. In 1983 the Northumberland Wildlife Trust took over the management and development of Hauxley. Paths and hides were constructed, reed beds developed, and trees planted, providing an excellent variety of habitats sandwiched between farmland to the west and the dunes to the east. Water levels can be adjusted at times of migration, leaving areas of mud that encourage waders. Careful management of other areas has encouraged both Little-ringed Plover and Reed Warbler to breed, as both spread their ranges northwards. It is one of the best sites to see red squirrel and there are increasing sightings of otter.

In recent years, Hauxley nature reserve has been extensively remodelled and extended and now has a state-of-the-art, eco-friendly visitor centre, toilets and café, built by volunteers. There is an educational area that hosts classes and events, a sightings information board with details from the reserve and other nearby areas such as East Chevington, Druridge Pools and Cresswell Ponds (see other sites p99). It is a good day's birdwatching to take in all four of these sites and the other habitats that lie next to the sea all along this stretch of coastline. For example a singing marsh warbler was present at Togston links for weeks and the entire area has several records for Black Redstart.

Visitors over the summer months can enjoy flowers including viper's bugloss, bloody cranesbill and northern marsh orchid. These attract a large variety of butterflies such as the common blue and wall brown. There are also dragonflies and damselflies on the ponds, including the common hawker and the common darter.

Another abstract study titled 'Herons at Hauxley'. Multi media painting that is part of the same 'kinetic' series painted in 2019. 'It was a very windy and wet day and two herons appeared to be preening while sheltering from high winds.'

It is estimated that over 60 species now breed on or around the reserve, with many more present as visitors during migration periods. Hauxley is an excellent and convenient mainland site to view terns and probably the most reliable on the east coast for the rare Roseate Tern that will often come to the reserve from their nearby breeding stronghold of Coquet Island. They will often join mixed groups of Arctic and Common Tern on a late summer afternoon to bathe in fresh water in front of the Tern Hide. A winter high tide brings waders off the shore and on to the reserve in a similar way to Snetisham in Norfolk, and, although numbers are not as impressive, they can include Turnstone, Purple Sandpiper, Knot and Bar-tailed Godwit.

This time of the year also brings in wintering sea duck such as Scaup and Long-tailed duck that will join sizeable parties of Wigeon, Mallard, Teal, Tufted Duck and perhaps the odd Pintail or even Smew that tend to commute between the various lakes up and down the length of Druridge Bay. The adjacent fields may have Whooper Swan and usually large flocks of Pink-footed Geese.

Another important habitat to this reserve is the shoreline itself, which can be explored at all times as it is not restricted to the reserve opening hours. The sea between the shore and Coquet Island is always productive and has a vast expanse of rocks revealed at low tide and a sheltered area of water that helps with identifying birds on the surface. This area can be excellent for divers, sea duck and Auks, while the shoreline will produce Rock Pipit, an often overlooked bird that is generally found foraging among the rocks and shingle for their diet of winged ants (Hymenoptera), aphids, small worms, sandhoppers and small marine mollusca. It is a much darker bird that the closely sized and similar Meadow Pipit. Visitors should not rule out Pied/White Wagtail here and possibly Snow Bunting in the winter months.

Look for Reed Warbler (left), now established in Druridge Bay. With a very similar song, they take some practice to separate from Sedge Warbler (right).

Timings

All year: Little Grebe, Mute Swan, Shelduck, Teal, Mallard, Grey Partridge, Pheasant, Moorhen, Coot, Ringed Plover, Lapwing, Redshank, Collared Dove, Skylark, Meadow Pipit, Rock Pipit, Pied Wagtail, thrushes, tits, corvids, Tree Sparrow, finches, Reed Bunting.

Spring: Kittiwake and gull passage, Canada Geese, Gadwall, Garganey, Ruddy Duck, passage waders, Ruff, Whimbrel, Greenshank, Green Sandpiper, Common Sandpiper, terns including Little and Black on passage. Gulls including Mediterranean and Little. Sabine's has been recorded. Cuckoo, hirundines, Ring Ouzel, Whinchat, redstart, Wheatear, Grasshopper, Sedge, Reed, Garden and Willow Warblers, Chiff-chaff, Blackcap and Spotted Flycatcher. Records for Spoonbill, Surf Scoter, Avocet, Temminck's Stint, Turtle Dove, Citrine Wagtail, Nightingale, thrush, Bluethroat, Icterine Warbler and Red-backed Shrike.

Late Summer - Autumn: Tape luring sessions for Storm Petrel, pictured, (details from the Northumbria ringing group), return waders with rarities that have included Pectoral Sandpiper, Terek Sandpiper, Marsh and White-rumped Sandpiper, Black-winged Pratincole, Ruddy Shelduck, Bridled Tern, Lesser-crested Tern, Lesser White-fronted Goose, Bar-headed Goose.

Storm Petrel.

Autumn (August-November): Passage of seabirds including terns and skuas. Red-breasted Merganser, Greylag and Barnacle Geese on passage. Waders including Curlew Sandpiper, Little Stint, Ruff, Spotted Redshank, Greenshank and Green Sandpiper. Increasing numbers of Ringed Plover, Sanderling and Dunlin.

October-November: Brings 'falls' of thrushes, Long-eared Owl, Short-eared Owl, Robin and Goldcrest. Twite and Snow Bunting to the beach with possible Lapland bunting and Shore Lark. Autumn rarities have included Hoopoe, Wryneck, Blyth's Reed Warbler, Icterine Warbler, Barred Warbler, Arctic Warbler, Buff-breasted Sandpiper, Marsh Warbler, Red-throated Pipit, Common Rosefinch, Little Bunting, Olive-backed Pipit, Paddyfield Warbler, Golden Oriole, Red-backed and Great Grey Shrike, Pallas's Warbler, Firecrest, Bonelli's Warbler and Arctic Redpoll.

Winter: Wintering divers and grebes often lingering until spring. Common and Velvet Scoter (sea), Smew, Goldeneye and sea duck, Peregrine, Merlin and Short-eared Owl, White Winged Gulls, Black Redstart has overwintered.

Access: Situated between High and Low Hauxley off the A1068, 1 mile south of Amble.There is ample car parking (charge) bird hides, disabled toilets, baby changing facilities, shop, cafe, picnic area and Wi-fi. Disabled access. Entry free but donations are welcomed. A track leaves the minor road between Low and High Hauxley. The entrance is shared with the caravan park.

Opening times
The Wildlife Discovery Centre and Reserve and Lookout Café are open at different times throughout the year. Check online for details.

Please do not climb on the mounds, as this will cause disturbance to the birds.

Other wildlife: The woods surrounding the car park have regular red squirrel. Flowers are also abundant at the reserve in the summer months, including kidney vetch, vipers bugloss and bloody cranesbill.

Tree Sparrow.

East Chevington.

Additional Sites

Boulmer

The site is probably best viewed as part of a day trip that perhaps takes in the Alnmouth estuary and Craster. Take the minor road north from the roundabout in Alnmouth. At the first T junction turn right. This road leads to Boulmer. An excellent view of the bay can be enjoyed from the rear of the Fishing Boat Inn (Food served - entrance through the pub).

A few rarities over the years (Hoopoe amongst others), but is best for waders on the incoming tide. Dunlin, Redshank, Curlew Sandpiper and Little Stint on migration. Bar-tailed Godwit can usually be seen, with Ringed Plover, Grey Plover and other shore birds. Check the shore areas of seaweed for Yellow Wagtail, Wheatear etc., and the bushes and trees along the lane to Craster for migrants such as Yellow-browed Warbler. Always interesting.

Craster

The Arnold Memorial Reserve below Craster Heugh, a whinstone outcrop, was set up in 1973 in memory of Dr Lawrence Arnold on land sold by Sir John Craster to the Northumberland Wildlife Trust. Its ex-quarry workings, secondary Blackthorn scrub, gorse and woodland, together with its position next to the coast makes the reserve particularly important for both migrant and breeding birds. Breeding bird species include sedge and Willow Warbler, Chiffchaff and Blackcap. Among the migrants a number of rarities have been recorded, including Wryneck, Icterine, Reed and Barred Warblers, Red-breasted Flycatcher and Bluethroat.

Cresswell Ponds

Formed since 1958 as a result of mining subsidence, Cresswell Ponds are comprised of one large brackish water-lagoon (the only permanent brackish water-lagoon on the Northumberland Coast) and two smaller freshwater areas. The main pond is connected to the sea by a short outfall stream which allows an in-flow of seawater leading to variations in both water levels and salinity in the lagoon during some high tides. The reserve, which is owned by

Alcan Farms is a SSSI and is managed by the Northumberland Wildlife Trust. It is one of several reserves that lie behind the sand dunes of Druridge Bay and by combining this site with nearby East Chevington, Druridge Bay pools and Country Park, Hauxley, the river Coquet and Coquet Island it is possible to plan a superb and varied birdwatching outing. Druridge Bay remains a beautiful and natural landscape and is now the site of a Harvest Mouse Release Programme, run in conjunction with Northumberland Wildlife Trust and Newcastle University.

Dunstanburgh Cliffs

The area around Dunstanburgh Castle (featured in three paintings by Turner) is both a SSSI and an AONB. The cliffs here are made of hard Whin Sill basalt rock. This promontory provides a home to the largest colony of Kittiwakes in Northumberland and it is possible to view most of the sea bird species on the nearby Farne Islands without leaving land.

Breeding: Fulmar, kittiwake (over 500 pairs), Puffin (scarce, scan cliff top), Razorbill, Guillemot and Shag. Wheatear, Stonechat, Yellow Wagtail and rarities have been recorded.

Druridge Pools and East Chevington

Druridge pools and East Chevington nature reserve were established from reclamation of the extensive open cast workings that existed in Druridge bay in the 1970s. They now form a link between Hauxley to the north and Cresswell ponds to the south. The whole Druridge Bay area is now totally reclaimed with the East Chevington reserve promising to be a superb coastal reedbed. It is hoped that Marsh Harrier (now breeding), Bittern and Bearded Tit will all become regular breeding species. However, large numbers of waders and wildfowl are present right along the entire stretch of this coastline in winter, with many species commuting between the various sites including regular Smew, Scaup, Pintail, Wigeon, Teal, Shoveler, Long-tailed Duck, Goldeneye, Whooper Swan and Pink-footed Geese. Lapwing and Golden plover are often joined by over-wintering Ruff.

Hen Harrier (particularly around Chevington moor, which is now a virtually guaranteed site for Barn Owl and Buzzard). Short-eared Owl and Merlin are often present, as well as Twite and Tree Sparrow, with mixed flocks of finches and buntings. Lapland and Snow Bunting can also be found. Recent rarities include Glossy Ibis. The information centre at Hauxley has a latest sightings board, but the area is well watched so anything of note usually gets passed along the 'birder's grapevine'.

Harwood forest

Harwood forest is owned by the Forestry commision and is a working forest. That said, it is possible to walk for miles here without encountering any forestry work. For variety, it is probably better to walk around Thrunton Woods or Holystone (upper Coquetdale). I have personally checked out this forest numerous times for Nightjar (mentioned in *Where to Watch Birds in North East England*) but have never found any, nor have I ever found Black Grouse (in over twenty years). The most interesting areas remain the young two to three-year-old stands of small conifers. In summer Whinchat, Cuckoo and Willow Warbler are a delight, and in winter there is regular Hen Harrier.

Common Buzzard and Sparrowhawk should be seen, and possibly Goshawk. As with most coniferous woodlands, Siskin, Chaffinch, Woodpigeon, Woodcock and Goldcrest breed in good numbers, with the latter three species virtually absent in winter, being replaced with 'winter thrushes' such as Redwing and Fieldfare.

About the Author

MiE (Mike Fielding) was born in
Darlington, County Durham, and as a
child moved to the town of Barnard
Castle. 'If I close my eyes, I can still see
my first bird - a beautiful male
Yellowhammer which was sitting on top
of a hedgerow in the evening sunshine
along Green Lane'. I was 8 years old.

From that moment Mike was hooked on birds and he has drawn, painted
and watched them ever since. 'When my parents moved to the then large
town of Sunderland, before it was designated a city, I remember accidentally
disturbing a Corn Bunting from it's nest on a rough grassland field directly
behind the school I attended - that was the 70s, and the memory of that bird
and its subsequent struggle has stayed with me throughout my life'.

At 16 he became the YOC local leader (the youth branch of the RSPB) for
County Durham and would organise trips to the county's birdwatching sites.
Often enthusiastically ringing the late Brian Unwin with his sightings. Mere
Knolls Cemetery which, due to its proximity to the coast, was an excellent
spot for migrants and became Mike's patch where he recalls the excitement
of his first Great-grey Shrike, Wryneck, Ring Ouzel and Long-eared Owl.

At this time Northumberland had a bird club so Mike and few friends
suggested to Brian Unwin that he looked into forming a club of the same
stature and later that same year the Durham Bird Club was formed.

Mike attended Sunderland College of Art & Design where he studied
environmental design and fine art as well as pursuing his other great love -
music. In the late 80s Mike turned his interest in birding into a full-time
business which was to eventually evolve into birdersmarket.com. His avant-
garde music outfit dumdum SCORE released the critically acclaimed album
Audio Sheep, extracts of which were featured by the ground breaking *Audio
Arts Magazine* and now archived at The Tate Modern.

On moving to Warkworth he wrote and illustrated *The Birds of Coquetdale*
in 2000. He is an active environmental campaigner, RSPB species sponsor,
fundraiser and co-author of *The Closest thing to Heaven* which looks at the
Newcastle music scene of the 70s & 80s. Mike now lives in the village of
West Thirston overlooking the River Coquet with his wife and daughter.
Further details can be found at www.voert.digital/mie

References

Anderson-Graham, P: *Highways and Byways of Northumbria* (1920) Macmillan and company. Reprinted 1973 E,J Morton.

Archer, David: *Land of Singing Waters*. Rivers and great floods of Northumbria Spreddon Press.

Beckensall, S.: *Northumberland Viewpoints*. Amberley 2010

Bennet, Linda: *A Guide to Nature Reserves of Northern England* 1989.

Britton, D and Day, J.C.: *Where to Watch Birds in North-East England*. Helm 1985

Cramp, S and Brooks, D.J.: *Handbook of the Birds of Europe the Middle East and North Africa. Volume VI Warblers*. OUP 1992

Day J.C and Charlton B.C.: *The Otterburn Estate. The Adjutant Journal of the Army Birdwatching Society volume 9*

Day J.C., Hodgson M.S. and Rossiter N.: *The Atlas of Breeding Birds in Northumbria*. NTBC 1995

Dickson W.: *Wildflowers of the Northumbrian Coast*. Keepdate Publishing 2000

Dixon D.D.: *Upper Coquetdale, Northumberland. Its history, traditions, folklore and scenery. 1903*

Dymond J.N., Frater P.A. and Gantlett S.J.M.: *Rare Birds in Britain and Ireland* T& AD Poyser 1989

Galloway, B. and Meek, E.R.: *Northumberland's Birds Parts 1,2 & 3*. Natural History Society of Northumbria 1983

Geldard, E.: *Northumberland and the Land of the Price Bishops*. Breedon Books 2008

Honeyman, Herbert L.: *Northumberland*. Robert Hale Ltd 1949

McCandrews, T.L.: *Amble and District. History, Geology and Botany*. W G Chambers (Sandhill Press 1997)

Morrison, P. and Rylance, G.: *Coquet Island, Northumberland*. Belfry Publicity 1989

Northumberland Wildlife Trust: *Nature Reserves of the Northumberland Wildlife Trust* 1976

Northumberland County History Committee (Madeline Hope-Dodds ed): *A History of Northumberland Volume XV; The Parish of Simonburn, Rothbury and Alwinton*. Northumberland and Durham Naturalists Trusts Ltd. *Harbottle Crags* 1970

O'Connor, R.J. and Shrubb, M.: *Farming and Birds*. Cambridge University Press 1990

Pritchard, D.E. et al: *Important Bird Areas in the UK including the Channel Islands and the Isle of Man*. RSPB 1992

Stevens J.N. and M.: *The Hidden Places of Northumberland and Durham*. M & M Publishing 1992

Story, Richardson and Wylam (eds): *Clippings Upper Coquetdale volume 2*. Upper Coquetdale Publications

Tyler E.G.: *The Birds of Upper Coquetdale, Their present status and distribution 1938-1947*. Trans of the Natural History Society of Northumberland, Durham and Newcastle-Upon Tyne volume XI

Watson, Godfrey: *Northumberland Villages*. Robert Hale London 1976

Wright G.N.: *The Northumbrian Uplands*. David & Charles 1989

Useful Addresses

Alnwick Tourist Information Centre & Library, The Playhouse, Bondgate Without, Alnwick NE66 1PQ. 01670 622152

Arriva Bus Services www.arriva.co.uk/north-east/places/amble

Otterburn Live Firing Times
www.gov.uk/goverment/publications/otterburn-firing-times

Northumberland National Park www.northumberlandnationalpark.org.uk

Dave Gray Puffin Cruises (For Coquet Island) 01665 711975 operating from Amble Quayside.

Northumberland Wildlife Trust https://www.nwt.org.uk

Hauxley Nature Reserve Discovery Centre. Near Low Hauxley village, Low Hauxley Northumberland NE65 0JR

Northumberland Gazette, 32 Bondgate Without, Alnwick, Northumberland NE66 1PN 01665 602234
www.northumberlandgazette.co.uk

Royal Society for the Protection of Birds, The Lodge, Sandy, Bedfordshire www.rspb.org.uk

Northumberland and Tyneside Bird Club www.ntbc.org.uk

National Trust Cragside, www.nationaltrust.org.uk/cragside 01669 620333

Northumberland Coastguard
www.facebook.com/HMCoastguardNorthumberland/

Full Northumberland birdwatching site guide at www.birdersmarket.com